Entertainment Is A

GOD

Eyedea

jo'EL

Entertainment Is A

GOD

Eyedea

The Handbook for Hollywood

Entertainment Is A God Eyedea

© Copyright 2016-jo'EL

jo'EL

P.O. Box 5828

Oceanside Ca. 92054

Email: joel@joelturman.com

www.1joel.com

ISBN-13:978-0692643495 (Dreams Now)

ISBN-10:0692643494

Printed in the United States of America by jo'EL

Endorsements

Entertainment is a God Eyedea is a book written for many who have felt a pull from God to enter the world of Entertainment. In the past, the world of "Hollywood" and God did not like one another was the attitude of most people. Because Christian people stayed away, the darkness led the way. Now there has come a new generation that is called and carries a strong mandate from God to help bring Christian support to this powerful influence throughout the world. jo'EL has written a clear and powerful book to help guide and to help understand the role of God in Entertainment. This is a book worth your time to read.

Roberts Liardon, Sarasota, Florida

Author of *God's Generals, The Price of Spiritual Power, God's Generals for Kids*

"By understanding that entertainment is a way to manifest the Word of God and bring the presence of His Glory, Pastor jo'EL Turman brings a different perspective to entertainment that empowers Christians who operate in that sphere of influence. Just as important, he offers a new insight into the identity of our God and His will for us." –

Greg Wallace, Apostolic Ambassador, Harvest International Ministry

Author of *Transforming: The Power of Leading From Identity*

Entertainment is a God Eyedea is a trumpet call full of transformational strategy! This book is real, relatable and revelatory...I was engaged from the first page. I agree with jo'EL when he says "I believe that just like the Renaissance (which rebirthed the church by the reformers of that day) the next Move of God will come through the influence of the Arts and Entertainers of our time."

Spring Huemme, His House

Author of *I am a Child of God - Declarations for Children and Kings Decree*

It is a pleasure to do an Endorsement for Apostle jo'EL for his brand new book *Entertainment is a God Eyedea*. I love the fresh perspective that jo'EL brings regarding reaching into the darkest places of society and showing them the marvelous light and love of Christ. This book will both challenge and inspire you to believe God for greater things in your own walk with

Him. It will cause faith to rise in your heart for bringing reformation and revival to every sphere of influence in the world around you.

Jerame Nelson, Living At His Feet Ministries

Author of *Burning Ones: Calling Forth a Generation of Dread Champions, Activating Your Spiritual Senses and more*

For a number of years I have known of jo'EL Turman's passion for impacting the realm of Arts and Entertainment with the Gospel of Jesus Christ. Now I understand why. Having been in the throes of the music industry as a young man, he was exposed to the elusive quest for fame with all of its trappings. Life in this industry without God as your anchor can be frustrating at best and devastating at its worst. In *Entertainment is a God Eyedea*, this author gives us a behind the scenes look at the personal cost of pursuing a realm of fame and glory that can only be safely accessed through the God of Glory. Indeed, we have all been made in the image of God in order to be great as a reflection of His Glory. But when glory is pursued in the flesh apart from God, the consequences can be fatal. Go on a journey with jo'EL as he describes the origin and the original intent of Entertainment and shows us how we can redeem this great social medium for the God of Glory. Be prepared to be enlightened and challenged.

Apostle Eric L. Warren

Apostle and Senior Elder of Equippers City Church,
Columbus, Ohio

Author of *The Seven Spirits of God, Consider Your Ways and more*

Dedication

I dedicate *Entertainment is a God Eyedea* to my family, who are always the ultimate inspiration for me to do what I do. My wife and kids are so important and precious to me. They push me without saying a word to fulfill all that God has called me to be and do. My desire to touch the world comes from the love I see in their eyes for me and the belief that they put in me. The creativity my wife walks in and the trust I have in her to have my back is enormous.

My wife Lupita always has a heart that totally leans toward me going for whatever the Lord has put in my heart. She gives me space and time to create without any stress; for that I'm forever grateful. My kids are so amazing I don't even know where to start. They are so giving toward the call I have on my life they also make it easy for me to work. All of my family is creative and they help out quite a bit with ideas on a regular basis. Without a doubt their love keeps me on track.

To my parents who have always believed in me, I love you, I love you, I love you. Since I can remember you have spoken into my life and imparted to me that I can do whatever

I put my mind to. Mom, thank you for making me read summer after summer and giving me a love to read. It's only natural that I would write a book after how many I've read! My only regret is that it took me this long to write my first one. However, the first one is the hardest, now I know I can do it. Watch out now!

To my brothers and sister, thank you for respecting what I've been called to do. Lord knows there have been many times of disagreement during our lives - but man - there have been so many more times of laughing and enjoying each other's presence. You all help keep me focused because we are all so competitive. I feel like I have to succeed because my siblings are a success; I can't be the only slouch in the family! Ha Ha! You all provoke me to greatness in a good way - your support has always been more than I can put a price on. Thank you!

A c k n o w l e d g e m e n t s

I want to thank Joy Morga for editing the book for me with speed and excellence. You truly are the greatest of all because you carry a true servant's heart. You made a somewhat scary process a lot more comfortable and you are a joy to work with. Your name fits you well. Phillip DeLacruz, my go to man, thank you for the emergency cover and all the work you've done for me in the past, your talent is off the charts. Andre Radar, thanks for the artwork and being there for me. You have been a steady source of creativity in my life. Since we were kids you have been super creative and you continue to surprise me with your talent and gifting.

Spring, you are the best girlfriend a guy can have. Thank you for stepping out and writing your books. We encourage each other all the time but you are extremely supportive of me and such a joyful source of the life of God. I can't help but stay focused on advancing the Kingdom with you around. I appreciate you big time. To all my mentors, moms and pops in the Spirit: Apostle Eric Warren, David Hogan, Greg and Linda Wallace, Dr. Mark Barclay, Bishop Hernandez and Bishop Blackmon - your leadership is an example that created an easy pathway for me to follow. Roberts Liardon, your advice and help in this project and your push for me to write a book - no I take that back - to write at least 10 books, was just what I needed! Praise God, I have at least 9 more to go! Becca Greenwood, you are a cornerstone to my life and ministry. You have no idea how huge that is to me and to my family. Thank you all.

To all my friends in the ministry who surround me with encouragement and a culture of success - I understand the love David felt towards Jonathon in the love I have for you. Craig Muster, Jerame Nelson, Shawn Bolz, Sean Smith, Angela Greenig, Scott Anthony, Steve Kasyanenko, Mark McElwee, Tamara Lowe, Priscilla and Mike Guthrie, Darren Thomas and Daniel Jones, I appreciate you all.

Last but not least I have to give a huge thank you, thank you, thank you to the His House Family. You are the best church I could ever want to lead! I not only have people who love me as a leader but also people who love me as a friend and brother in the Lord. It's our time. We can change the world!

Contents

Foreword

As I read jo'EL's book, *Entertainment is a God Eyedea,* I found myself pulled into his subject in a way I didn't expect. He does something unusual in blending his experience as a Christian and artist with the "Arts Mountain"…or that's how those of us in the Seven Mountain or 7m world would describe this arena. Think of the power of the Arts and Entertainment Mountain to shape the ideas and aspirations of young people and social movements. Who are the heroes and role models of the next generation? Think about the singers, sports stars, actors and actresses and their influence on culture. In the 7m world, Arts are the Sabbath Mountain. Think of it – every other mountain exists in every culture because of necessity. All these are needed: Family, Education, Business, Government, Media, even Faith…but Arts? It isn't a necessity; not really. Arts are a gift to mankind. It's the place of renewal and inspiration. That is why it's the Sabbath Mountain – it is made for man.

jo'EL takes us up this mountain and gives us a glimpse of how it can either be a gift or a grief – depending on who the artist is. Let us never forget that according to Ezekiel 28:13, lucifer was uniquely designed: "every precious stone was thy covering" and "the workmanship of your timbrels and of your pipes was prepared in you in the day that you were created." Timbrels (tabrets) are tambourines or percussion sounds; pipes are literally "holes" as in all wind instruments – trumpets, great cathedral organs and flutes. lucifer was built with the capacity to conduct and orchestrate as well as participate in the worship of Heaven! As worship swelled up into a crescendo lucifer (whose name means "shining one" or "light bearer") would ignite into a cosmic explosion of multicolored glory accompanied with a celestial symphony of sound! He would then beam this display of glory back to the throne that he covered like a canopy of glory. And all this continued, we know not how long, until the day he became aware of his beauty and gifts and wondered why he himself was not more exalted.

What became of this musical and visual creative gift? When this artistic expression was cast out of heaven it was not reassigned to other angels. The privilege of exalted worship and glorious artistic expression was given to another species – the children of men. This is why I am so enthused to see jo'EL take on this subject! There are many counterfeits of this glory on the earth but the hour is coming when Heaven's Musicians, Songwriters, Playwrights, Illustrators, Fashion Designers and Architects will shine as only the once "anointed" cherub could shine. For this reason, hell has a particular malice towards artists because they take the place of the fallen angel – who Ezekiel said "had the seal of perfection, full of wisdom and perfect in beauty." This seal and sum is now transferred and revealed in the Bride of Christ - the ultimate beauty, drawn out of the wounded side of Jesus Himself. In light of all this, jo'EL has done us a great service by reigniting our vision of the Arts and the high calling of Artists. You will enjoy this highly readable work.

Dr. Lance Wallnau Director of the Lance Learning Group

The Catalyst behind the 7 Mountain (7m) Message. "Destiny Dashboard", "Doing Business Supernaturally", www.lancewallnau.com

Foreword

I remember when I was first open with Christian friends that I wanted to impact the Entertainment Industry. They laughed in judgement and criticized me for wanting to do something so worldly. I watched, as these same people had a very dysfunctional relationship to entertainment - watching sports and listening to music - they didn't have a grid for why entertainment is God's idea first. God's first identity revealed in the Bible is Creator. He is the most entertaining being to ever exist! He loves to capture and hold the attention of humanity. So many next generation leaders, pastors and children of well-known Christians are feeling the call to go after a career in entertainment. They are feeling the same sense of calling that the previous generation of Christians felt to build the church. Why? God wants to use popular culture to bring his Kingdom Culture.

In *Entertainment Is A God EyeDea*, jo'EL takes you on a journey that is both personal and theological. He helps us to bridge the relationship of faith and entertainment. He outlines the strategy of the enemy but connects our full hope to the one who owns it all, Jesus.

I am so encouraged that my Brother (who grew up as a rapper in the hood but ended up becoming a leader among leaders) leverages his great perspective for all of us to grow from. This book is a building block towards developing a bridge between the church and the industry that has been neglected and sometimes avoided by the very Fathers and Mothers who lead Christianity today.

If you are an Entertainer - read it and get a download of faith! If you are a Christian with a complicated relationship towards entertainment - read it and get reprogrammed! If you are a Church Leader, realize as you read it that God is giving us entertainment as the most significant harvesting and maturing tool in history! The next great revival will be marked by our impact and use of the Entertainment Industry!

Shawn Bolz, Founding Pastor of Expression58 Church in Los Angeles

Author of *Translating God* www.bolzministries.com

Introduction

Let me quickly grab your attention with two points of view blowing around where entertainment is concerned. I'm going to start first with the "sky is falling syndrome" constantly gusting through our lives every day. Then I'm going to take you into "the eye of the storm" where I believe God is peacefully looking at our entertainment.

As we look around, the winds of change seem to be blowing out of control in America at hurricane speeds. This hurricane is forcefully bending the trees of our morality, causing them to snap under the pressure. It is knocking over the power lines of our faith where compromise is concerned. This dangerous storm system has moved upon the beaches of our lives into the cities and countryside of our existence. Shattering the windows of our soul, the gust of cold air has penetrated our government, schools, businesses, families and the way our media operates. It has blown the frigid air even into our churches. The name of this hurricane is not Sandy, Ike, Andrew or even Katrina. This hurricane has been named "Hurricane Entertainment."

While society runs for cover from the flying debris of escalating violence that smashes into our daily routines, people scream for help. They look for relief from the winds that seem to be blowing at us from every direction. The waters from the tempest have flooded our streets with police brutality, anxiety from the constant push of negative news reports, homicides, riots and men who pay more attention to fantasy football than to their families. The streets are flooded with women trying to look like pop stars and actresses who spend thousands of dollars to get breast and butt implants, Botox and plastic surgery of all kinds. People are drowning in debt through the ever present urge to have the latest gadget, cell phone, bigger television and better computer.

The streets are flooded with promiscuity among our children who see sexual scenes and references every day through smart phones, iPads, television, laptops, etc. They now have access to xxx-rated content at the push of a button. Let's not forget about the deterioration of marriage and extremely high paid athletes with low righteous values. Oh my friends, the list can go on and on, I'm sure you get the picture. Most people wait on an answer - like someone sitting on top of the roof looking for someone in a boat to rescue them from contaminated waters rising higher and higher. The answers to the enormous problems caused by Hurricane Entertainment are in the "Eye of the Storm." That's right, in the Eye of the Storm. If you look from an aerial view, right in the middle of every hurricane there is what is called "the eye of the storm." In this eye, the storm is calm, the winds are very low and it's mostly sunny. Ha Ha! Right in the middle of Hurricane Entertainment there is an eye - I'm going to say for this metaphor, "God's eye." This is the place in the storm where it is calm, peaceful and there is hope, Christ in us, the Hope of Glory.

satan did not create entertainment. No, he is standing like a big bad wolf, huffing and puffing, kicking up winds to try to blow God's house down. As I refer to his wicked attempts to own entertainment, I'm going to call his storm front Hurricane Entertainment - to separate it from God's purpose for his Eyedea of Entertainment. Speaking of Eyedea, allow me to extract the eye out of the hurricane metaphor for a minute, to use this analogy to point out the solution to most of the problems we face where entertainment is concerned.

I'm using the eye because most of the time, the answer to our problems is in our perspective of how we perceive the very problem we are facing. In other words, is the glass half full or half empty? The glass half empty is a problem, the glass half full is a blessing. You see, we can look at a rose bush and be upset that the rose bush has thorns, or, be happy that the thorn bush has roses. In every problem, there is a promotion waiting! A courageous person will pick up the problem and press into the Holy Spirit for wisdom - so that the promise behind the problem can come to pass.

Let's look for a moment at the story in the Bible where Jesus and his disciples were caught in a terrible storm with gale force winds. While the storm was blowing and the disciples were afraid, Jesus was asleep. His eyes where closed; he was not looking at what the disciples were looking at. I believe that while Jesus was asleep, he saw images from the Holy Spirit - the eyes of the disciples saw the boat being flooded with water. The disciples saw a problem and Jesus saw peace. The eyes of Jesus saw heaven and his heart was flooded with peace. Out of the abundance of the heart his mouth spoke. Out of the abundance of a heart full of peace, Jesus woke up and said "Peace, be still." Let me back up a bit to catch this very important point. Jesus was asleep because he understood the purpose of the storm. He did not cause the storm, he understood that things that come against us are an opportunity for us. For the disciples in this story it was an opportunity to exercise their faith. This is why when he rebuked the storm he asked the disciples, "Where is your faith?"

Praise God! If we can understand the purpose of entertainment we can use the winds from Hurricane Entertainment for our benefit! Like Jesus, we must refuse to run around afraid looking to hide ourselves. We must position ourselves in the "Eye of the Storm" right in the middle, like Shammah.

> **2 Samuel 23:11, 12** *Next to him was Shammah son of Agee the Hararite. When the Philistines banded together at a place where there was a field full of lentils, Israel's troops fled from them. But Shammah took his stand in the middle of the field. He*

defended it and struck the Philistines down, and the Lord brought about a great victory,

Shammah, who defended himself against the Philistines, positioned himself in the middle of a field full of lentils. Catch this, my friends, Shammah positioned himself in the middle of a field of lentils, but Esau sold his birthright for lentil soup!

> **Genesis 25:31-34** *And Jacob said, Sell me this day thy birthright. And Esau said, Behold, I am at the point to die and what profit shall this birthright do to me? And Jacob said, Swear to me this day; and he sware unto him: and he sold his birthright unto Jacob. Then Jacob gave Esau bread and pottage of lentils and he did eat and drink, and went his way; thus Esau despised his birthright.*

What one person will sell his birthright for another will position himself right in the middle of it to defend it. So, instead of us selling our birthright to possess entertainment, let's position ourselves in the middle of this storm where the eye is and take back what the devil stole. My friends, helping the body of Christ get in position to win and take back entertainment is the reason I'm writing this book. I feel the Holy Spirit wants to help us see from God's eye. This is from a position higher than the storm, where we tap into Papa's vision for entertainment and realize that, **Entertainment is a God Eyedea.**

Chapter One

What is the Meaning of all This?

IT WAS A FAIRLY COOL SUMMER night in southern California as I looked out the window at passing traffic. Now I know in comparison to most places it's very cool but for us spoiled folks who live in San Diego County, we were just getting over a bit of a heat wave. The last two days the temperature had reached a hot 85 degrees with humidity peaking at 97%; so to us that night was fairly cool☺. We were enjoying the small break in the heat the night brought but still looking for a cool place to just hang out and relax. What better place than a cool movie theater with some good Hot Buttered Popcorn, Red Vines, Sprite and an entertaining flick?

My Inner Battle

We were on our way to see the movie War Room. I had not heard of it at all other than my mother giving it rave reviews. After I saw it I knew why. My mother could have played the part of the Prayer Warrior Miss Clara with ease. Our friend Spring blessed my wife and I with tickets to see the movie. On the way out, she said the movie was the story of my Mother, Dorothy Turman, and her. Anyways, let me back up to before I went into the theater. I knew nothing about War Room other than it was a Christian movie and that I had seen other movies from the same producers. I thought it would be good. Oh wow, was I in for a treat. That movie was amazing!

While sitting in the somewhat empty theater I laughed, cried, cheered and even praised God out loud. How many times do you get to do that in a movie? The feeling of being at the movies with strangers didn't occur to me; it felt like the people there were family. Then I had a flashback of the audience of a different movie I had recently seen. Now, I'm not a big movie goer - no - I'm a Redbox, Netflix kind of guy. My biggest expense for a movie usually is forgetting to take the Redbox movie back, errrrggggg! What I'm saying here is, I don't see many movies in theaters but in a matter of weeks, I saw two movies (unusual for me.) However, that's the exact reason I was able to quickly compare the two movies. Please allow me to dive into the battle I was now having in my mind.

I had watched the movie Straight Outta Compton, but in light of seeing the glorious movie War Room, my spirit stirred to dig deeper into the trenches of prayer. I thought about how could I have ever wanted to see Straight Outta Compton? The fact that I traveled with Eazy E as a rap artist (up until Eazy went into the hospital and died) was a contributing factor. My role in Da I.B.S. (Innocent Bystanders) for sure played a major part. But my perplexity stretched me further than that thought. I did not see trailers or billboards for War Room but saw many for Straight Outta Compton. No, as I sat and looked at a theater that was less than 10% filled, I again spun into thoughts of the impact Hurricane Entertainment was having on our society from a Christian vs. Secular comparison.

As I went home, I began to look at the amount of money made by both films during their opening weekend. Straight Outta Compton brought in $60.2 million, War Room brought in 11.35 million. Now don't get me wrong, War Room is breaking records for faith-based films; at the time of writing this book, it is currently the number 2 movie (ahead of Mission Impossible.) However, when I look at the life changing content that is in War Room I'm stirred up! I thought Straight Outta Compton was a good movie in terms of entertainment but the images of nudity, the orgy scene, drugs and foul language definitely do nothing for the spirit; it leaves bruises on the soul. With this in mind, literally, I'm thinking how much and how long do these images affect me? How much and how long do these types of movies affect others? I mean I'm someone who gets into the word consistently, but when it comes to the renewing of the mind, how much do we go around the mountain? We plant tares then turn around and labor to pull them up, only to plant tares again the next time an opportunity arises to be entertained. It is this thought that drove me to study, search, seek, pray and ask God for wisdom to command "Peace Be Still" to Hurricane Entertainment.

Entertainment is Huge

When we take a look at entertainment the first thing we have to understand is that entertainment isn't just movies or music. Entertainment is not just what is produced by Hollywood. Now I'm sure when we think about this, we know it intellectually. However, most of the time when we talk about entertainment our focus has been largely directed towards places like Broadway, maybe even Las Vegas and especially Hollywood (where our movies, television shows and music predominantly come from.) Entertainment is more than that. It's our sporting events that attract thousands live on location and millions by broadcast. It's our video games - whether we are playing them on iPads, smart phones or computers. Entertainment is opera, paintings, sculptures, poetry, storytelling and the circus. Entertainment is Disneyland, Six Flags and all amusement parks. It's rolling a ball across the floor back and forth with our children. It can be watching rain run down the window as one drop merges with another. Entertainment is watching a magician perform tricks, going to a spelling bee and even public punishment. Entertainment is banquets, birthday celebrations, reading, parades, fireworks and even shopping. Some entertainment tends to be more educational so we call it "edutainment or infotainment." As you can see, there is a broad spectrum to what we call entertainment. So, let's break this down a little bit further to understand more "what is the meaning of all this?"

The origins of entertainment go all the way back to Ancient Egypt and further. We will get into that in the next two chapters. With that said, let me interject here that my goal for writing this book is not to give you a timeline of entertainment and when things were created. For example, in 1979, the Sony Walkman was sold, in 1941 we had our first Television broadcast in the United States, or even how in 1930, the Jukebox was marketed. I can tell you from looking it up that in 1877 the Phonograph was invented. That is not the purpose of this book. I want to give you insights to why Hurricane Entertainment is blowing so fiercely over our nation. To get a timeline, you can look it up yourself very easily. I want you to walk away from this book knowing, by understanding and revelation, that *Entertainment is a God Eyedea.*

Okay! Let me bring you the meat of this subject so you can start chewing on it like a well-seasoned steak from Outback. Are you ready? Yes? Good! I don't think you would have bought this book if you weren't ready or maybe even called to change and impact the Entertainment Industry. So, I pray right now that the Holy Spirit will anoint your mind to get revelation from what I'm about to share with you. I bind any demonic force that would try to stop what the Holy Spirit wants to do. Amen.

The Purpose is in the Definition

Here we go…. Entertainment is a form of activity that holds the attention and interest of an audience, or gives pleasure and delight. It can be an idea or a task. It is more likely to be an activity or event that has developed over thousands of years - specifically for the purpose of keeping the attention of an audience. If you look up the word entertainment in the dictionary you will see that the definition is: amusement or pleasure that comes from watching a performer playing a game etc., the act of amusing or entertaining people. This is why big parks built specifically for entertainment are called amusement parks.

Now let's go a little bit further and look at the etymology of the word "entertainment." Etymonline.com says the word means to keep up, maintain a certain frame of mind to hold together, stick together, support. It comes from the Latin word inter + tenir - "to hold" or "tenet." The word "tenet" is where we get the word "tenure," which is the amount of time someone holds a job. "Ten" from tenet means "to stretch." So when we entertain someone, we are holding their attention. To jump way ahead for a second, when we are entertained by God, our minds are stretched to contain more of him. When our mind is stretched, it cannot go back to the way it was before.

Before I put these pieces together like a puzzle so you can get the whole picture, let's look at one of the key words in the definition of entertainment. The key word used to describe entertainment is the word "amusement" or "amuse." Remember, the definition of entertainment is the amusement of a person. The definition of amusement is diversion, provided especially by performers, something diverting or engaging. Amuse means to entertain someone in a light and pleasant way; it also means to divert the attention of, so as to deceive. Amuse comes from the word "muse" which means to dream, to ponder or meditate on. This is the sweet spot of entertainment, right here… meditation. Meditation fixes our mind on one thing or entertains our mind on one thing. It diverts our attention from everything else. Hmmm, so when I'm being entertained by Blue Bloods (my favorite show,) there is a form of meditation that is diverting my mind from current problems or responsibilities.

Another word from the word muse is "bemuse," which means to make utterly confused. As we continue to dive into this subject remember, there is good and there is evil. There is the original intention of creation and the twisted version the demonic world tries to rule with. Before we go on, one more interesting definition I found is in the etymology of the word "sport," meaning, to take pleasure, to amuse oneself. (We will talk about that later.) This is why sports are entertainment. Ok, that was a freebie! I want you to pay attention to the words diversion and amusing as we pick up on how satan uses these words in the next chapter.

Notes

Chapter Two

See Spot Run

WHEEEE! WE ARE FINISHED with the definitions for a minute or two and I'm happy about it. I mean, I love getting into the meaning of words, the origin of a word tells you a lot - but show me how they connect. Then I can put those definitions to work for my understanding. You know what I mean? Ok, so let's do exactly that; let's connect the dots here as we move on. Let me first bring something to your attention: though satan is not my focus, this chapter will have a lot of references to what he would like to do or continue to do with entertainment. satan is a defeated foe; I believe shedding light on his tricks will cause his darkness to flee. Darkness with no other choice flees when you turn on the light. Hey now, we know when we turn on the light in a dark room what happens - the dark disappears. While the amount of darkness that goes away depends on how much light and the strength of the light; the darkness goes without any questions or arguments. What I'm saying is, I truly see the value of entertainment and the eye God has for it. I'm only pointing out what the devil is doing so we will be able to clearly see that the winds of Hurricane Entertainment that are causing destruction are not from God. So bear with me as I uncover satan's strategy for using entertainment the way he has.

As we move towards the eye of the hurricane we must not be distracted by the items flying by us. We must continue to keep our focus on what is in front of us. The items that fly by us in Hurricane Entertainment are things like texts, emails, games on our phone, Facebook, Snap Chat, Instagram, etc., and who knows what is to come. Hold up, hold up! I see heads already shaking like this is going to be one of those stay away from the world books. Well, I have good news, it's not! The idea of staying away from the world, particularly entertainment, is the exact reason for this book! For too long we as Christians have thrown the baby out with the bath water. We have tried to separate ourselves from what God gave people - the ability to create. So relax - Facebook, Video Games like Black Ops and Television shows like The Voice all have a place and time to enjoy. Bear with me as we walk through this.

What I want to convey to you is that for us to accomplish anything significant in life we must learn how to focus on the task or goals at hand, whether it is being a good parent, leading a major corporation or even becoming one of the number one actors or actresses in Hollywood.

Entertainment, as I will point out, plays a tremendous part in our ability to focus. If we are to stay focused it means our eyes are fixed on the goal. When record breaking Gold Medalist Michael Phelps was training for the Olympics, he devoted his time to training. We can clearly see the results of not looking to the left or right, not playing XBox or going to the movies while he was training. He won 18 Gold Medals! To focus we need to not look to the left or right, but consider the path we are taking. Does that sound familiar? That's Proverbs 4:25-27. Take a look...

> **Proverbs 4:25** *Let your eyes look straight ahead, And your eyelids look right before you.* **26** *Ponder the path of your feet, And let all your ways be established.* **27** *Do not turn to the right or the left; Remove your foot from evil.*

We are given instructions not to turn to the right or left right after God says to guard your heart with all diligence. Now, why would God tell us right after he says to guard our heart with all diligence for out of it spring the issues of life, to watch what we are looking at or focused on? God knows that whatever we look at we move towards. Do you remember when you were a little kid first learning how to ride a bicycle? You were pedaling and going straight - all of a sudden your friend called your name. You looked and as you turned your head, you and your bike slowly veered off in the direction you were looking. If you are like me, that landed you straight into the grass for an abrupt stop.

The devil also knows that if he can hold our attention or entertain us then he can direct which way we go. What we see, say and hear goes into our hearts as seed; whatever we plant shows up in our life. If we plant seeds of love we will see love spring up in our lives. If we plant seeds of violence or drama from reality shows we will see drama in our lives. This is how life works - whatever you sow you will reap.

satan is a Master at Distractions

Guard your heart with all diligence in what direction you're looking and do not be distracted. This is why satan is a "master at distractions," which is in the very definition of entertainment. Now if you think about the word distraction we can see, in a humorous but true way, distraction is where your traction becomes dissed, lol. If we use the metaphor of the Seven Mountains, (which was popularized by Lance Wallnau) when you're trying to climb the mountain to the top of your sphere of influence, and your traction becomes dissed or you lose traction, you begin to slide back down to the bottom. In Genesis 22:2 Abraham was told by God to sacrifice his Son Isaac. In Genesis 22:5 Abraham told the two young men who would be a distraction to wait here, Isaac and I will go worship God and come back to you.

> *Genesis 22:2* *Then He said, "Take now your son, your only son Isaac, whom you love, and go to the land of Moriah, and offer him there as a burnt offering on one of the mountains of which I shall tell you."*

> *Genesis 22:5* *And Abraham said to his young men, "Stay here with the donkey; the lad and I will go yonder and worship and we will come back to you."*

Abraham's focus - what he was seeing - was that he was going to go up the mountain and come back with Isaac. This meant that somehow, God was going to provide the sacrifice that Abraham needed to make. Abraham told the young men to wait because they were going to be a distraction from the purpose he was going up the mountain for.

There is another example, in the life of Jacob, of what happens when we focus, meditate and allow our minds to be entertained by God. Jacob made an interesting deal with Laban:

> **Genesis 30:32** *Let me go through all your flocks today and remove from them every speckled or spotted sheep, every dark-colored lamb and every spotted or speckled goat. They will be my wages.*

Jacob then took rods of green poplar and of the hazel and chestnut tree and peeled white streaks in them, and exposed the white which was in the rods. Then he set the rods in front of the flocks so when they came to drink they would conceive. The flocks conceived before the rods and brought forth offspring that was straight, speckled, and spotted. The animals gave birth to what they were looking at, what they were focused on - what they could see that was entertaining their mind. This is why the Bible says in Hebrews 12:2:

> **Hebrews 12:2 (AV)** *Looking unto Jesus the author and finisher of our faith; who for the joy that was set before him endured the cross, despising the shame, and is set down at the right hand of the throne of God.*

We have to be looking at Jesus so that He can author and finish our faith! When it comes to Hurricane Entertainment, we have to be like Jacob and put specific entertainment in front of us – intentionally - to get the results in life we are looking for. We let the spots and speckles of what entertains us guide us - like breadcrumbs on a trail - oftentimes leading us to an undesired destination. It doesn't have to be this way though. Like the animals in Jacobs's story, we must focus on the right spots in entertainment so we can run the race God has set before us with endurance. Praise God! In the middle of this storm, if we can spot God and keep our eyes fixed on him, the purpose for entertainment will guide us to success in our calling!

My friends, this is why the devil is so interested in entertainment. He knows that entertainment keeps our mind held captive to what we are looking at. Now a captive or captivated mind is not bad. What makes a captivated mind bad is what our mind is being held captive with.

> **2 Corinthians 10:4 (AV)** *(For the weapons of our warfare are not carnal, but mighty through God to the pulling down of strongholds;)* **5** *Casting down imaginations, and every high thing that exalteth itself against the knowledge of God, and **bringing into captivity every thought** to the obedience of Christ;*

God says in 2 Corinthians 10:5 for us to hold all our thoughts captive to the obedience of Christ. But satan comes to divert our attention from the word of God. He wants to distract us from looking unto Jesus and distract us from looking into the word which is like looking into a mirror. He knows if we look into the mirror of the word we will be transformed into what we see, which is the Christ in us.

> **2 Corinthians 10:5** *We demolish arguments and every pretension that sets itself up against the knowledge of God, and we take captive every thought to make it obedient to Christ.*

2 Corinthians 3:18 *But we all, with open face beholding as in a glass the glory of the Lord, are changed into the same image from glory to glory, even as by the Spirit of the Lord.*

Using Entertainment is One of satan's Biggest Strategies

This is where it gets real interesting. We know that entertainment means to amuse or divert. What we must understand is the definition for "divert" – an attack or faint that draws the attention and force away from the point of the principal operation. It is not in accident that entertainment means amusement and amusement means diversion of attention (which is especially true in military actions.) The demonic army we are up against knows that if they divert our attention in one place they can maneuver around us in another place. If they divert our attention to our cell phones, iPads, movies, music and everything else, they can sneak into our schools and our government.

Our enemy has become a master at distracting us with entertainment that does not profit us at all. Check out these statistics listed by Darren Hardy, Publisher of *Success Magazine*. The average 13 to 17-year-old exchanges 4,000 texts a month, one every six minutes they are awake. 53% of us report checking email while driving. 61% continue to check email on vacation. One study showed office workers check email up to 40 times per hour! 67% check their phone for messages, alerts and calls, even when they don't notice their phone ringing or vibrating. 75% admit to using their phone in the bathroom, 30% say they never go to the bathroom without their phone. 69% cannot go to bed without checking their inbox. 43% confessed to checking email in the middle of the night. 35% check their phone before getting out of bed and 38% routinely check email at the dinner table. We have not only lost our minds but our manners too! Douglas Rushkoff, an American Media Theorist, Writer, Novelist, Columnist, Lecturer and Documentarian, calls this Digiphrenia - which is digitally induced mental chaos. Our phones, PDAs and computers alone are entertaining us to the point of addiction. 66% have Nomophobia (which I think should be called no-mo-phone-fee-a,) the fear of being out of mobile phone contact. This tactical movement exhibited by Hurricane Entertainment is rooted of course in fear. We are afraid we will miss something so we stay glued to our sources of information. This is dangerous, because information is coming at us at an accelerated pace. Think about your email for a second - how many of us are swamped with emails? Information overload is causing us to be overwhelmed and the more overwhelmed we are, the more we search for a convenient distraction.

People are starved for love and looking to get it through attention. Darren Hardy also said "Social media and constant digital connection is the stuff of mindless entertainment for the masses, a means of feeling important for the chronically unimportant, distractions from an unsatisfactory real life." Ouch! When it comes to the overload of advertisement it is like the Rat Test. If a food pellet is distributed the same time all the time, the rat will only look for food at that specific time. If a food pellet is distributed at random times, the rat doesn't know when the reward is coming and is driven to check over and over again incessantly. Wow! How many of us check our phones first thing in the morning or even wake up during the night to check? Sounds like the "Rat Race" may have an alternate meaning.

satan Longs to Occupy Entertainment

Entertainment is a God Eyedea! Hurricane Entertainment is a storm agitated by satan, blowing out of control for our amusement. Let's look at the word amusement again. Amusement comes from the word "amuse" which means to divert the attention. Amuse also means to "beguile," to attract or interest someone. For example, "The Magician effortlessly beguiled and amazed the children." When we look at the etymology of beguile, one of the definitions is "ruse," which of course means to cause a diversion. Eve said in Genesis 3:13, the serpent beguiled her, in other words, deceived her.

> **Genesis 3:13** *Then the Lord God said to the woman, "What is this you have done?" The woman said, "The serpent beguiled me, and I ate."*

The devil's Form of Entertainment is a Deception

One more thing before we move on! The word amuse comes from the word muse, (which we will go into the next chapter.) Let's take a quick detour into some Greek Mythology. The Romans adopted the goddesses called the Muses which are the inspiration of Literature, Science and the Arts. The origins of the muses go back to Osiris, the Egyptian God who recruited them.

The Muses, the nine daughters of Zeus, were assigned to these functions: Calliope (Epic Poetry,) Clio (History,) Euterpe (Flutes and Lyric Poetry,) Thalia (Comedy and Pastoral Poetry,) Melpomene (Tragedy,) Terpsichore (Dance,) Erato (Love Poetry,) Polyhymnia (Sacred Poetry) and Urania (Astronomy.) This is very interesting to me! We know that Greek Mythology is man's explanation of gods through inspiration from demonic spirits or fallen angels. However, when we look at what satan is trying to do (by identifying the spirits) we see he is clearly showing his hand and giving us a clue to the characteristics of the spirits we are dealing with. satan wants to be God, he wants to be understood and worshiped. This causes him to give people ideas of what to write about him and his demonic angels. So as we look at entertainment and really break it down, we see that satan's plan is to divert and hold our attention using the arts and entertainment as we know it.

The muses clearly show that there is an intricate plan, a strategy from hell if you will, to cause us to focus on the wind and rain from Hurricane Entertainment and not God's Eyedea of what Entertainment should be. If the principalities, rulers of darkness and wicked spirits in the heavenly host can cause us to focus on the wind and waves it can cause us to sink. But, if we continue to look at what God is doing, we can walk on the waters of entertainment all the way into the arms of our Lord. Remember, satan is not a creator but an imitator. We can rest assured that if he is so interested in entertainment there is a plan by God that he is trying to counter attack. However, I see like in Jacob's flocks the spots marked with an X where there is treasure that lies in an earthen vessel. Be of good courage! God has a plan! Do not be moved by what you see. The things seen are temporary and subject to change (2 Corinthians 4:18).

> *2 Corinthians 4:18* *So we fix our eyes not on what is seen, but on what is unseen, since what is seen is temporary, but what is unseen is eternal.*

Notes

Chapter Three

God's Eyedea

NOW LET'S LOOK AT ENTERTAINMENT from the other point of view. Let's look from a Heavenly Perspective. Imagine - if we took our rightful positions (seated in heavenly places) how small Hurricane Entertainment would look. From a birds eye view in the sky, we would see God unraveling the plan for entertainment like Lazarus when he raised him from the dead. Let's go to Psalms, where praise is captured. Praise is important because praise lifts us above the storm. In the place of praise in Psalms 143:5, David gives us a picture of God's Eyedea of Entertainment.

> **Psalms 143:5** *I remember the days of old, I meditate on all thy works, I **muse** on the works of thy hands.*

The word "muse" here means to ponder, converse with oneself, commune, declare, meditate, pray, speak and talk with. There it is right there – entertainment! To be amused, to muse, is a God Eyedea! God wants us to meditate, think, commune and ponder what He has done. David was being entertained by the works of God's hands!

> **Joshua 1:8** *This book of the law shall not depart out of thy mouth but thou shalt meditate therein day and night that you may observe to do according to all that is written therein. For then you shall make thy way prosperous, and then thou shalt have good success.*

Meditation is Entertainment

The word meditate is the Hebrew word "hagah" which means to utter, muse, meditate, plot and speak. I love it! God said if you meditate or muse on my words day and night you will observe or see yourself doing it and then nothing can stop you - you will make your way prosperous. Can you see why the devil doesn't want you being entertained or amused by God? Check out what Timothy says:

> **1 Timothy 4:15** *Meditate on these things; give yourself entirely to them, that your progress may be evident to all.*

OMG! That's it right there! He said if you meditate on the word which is God (John 1:1) everyone will see your progress!

> **John 1:1** *In the beginning was the Word, and the Word was with God, and the Word was God.*

Picture your mom, your teacher, your husband or wife, your boss, your coach, etc.; everyone will see your progress. A better translation of the word used for progress is profit. God said if you let me entertain you I will cause you to profit. Huh, now that's different. How much money does Hurricane Entertainment blow out of our hands year in and year out? First, let's look at an actual hurricane. Hurricane Isaac in 2000 did damage to the tune of 1.5 Billion dollars. However, in that same year America spent over 200 Billion in Entertainment. Entertainment is big business and usually, we are on the spending end of it. But get this, God said that if you let me entertain you, I will not cost you money but I will cause you to profit. Now I don't know about you but that sounds good to me.

Now I know I have put a lot of emphasis up until now on the effects that Hurricane Entertainment has had on our nation and world and how God wants us to be entertained by him. Let me point out now that entertainment isn't restricted to meditating on the word. In the pure sense of the word entertainment, I have shown by definition and etymology that it is the mind being held or attention being captivated for pleasure. At the same time, entertainment (even in the general way we think of as sports, music or movies) is a God Eyedea. Even the earliest form of entertainment, which is storytelling, comes straight out of the Bible. The Prophet Joel said this regarding telling stories:

> ***Joel 1:2*** *Hear this, you elders, And give ear, all you inhabitants of the land! Has anything like this happened in your days, Or even in the days of your fathers?* ***3*** *Tell your children about it, Let your children tell their children, and their children another generation.*

I can just see families sitting around the fire telling stories – how God showed himself strong to deliver them from Pharaoh by opening up the Red Sea! How David killed a Giant that was 9 feet tall and had 6 fingers! Storytime for them had as much action and drama as our blockbuster movies today. Let's look at more examples in the Bible of Entertainment.

Sit back for a second and picture Jesus - if He wasn't quite the Entertainer I don't know who is! Jesus went from house party to house party lol. One house party (well, maybe not a house party but a wedding reception) he attended had wine and probably dancing and singing - yep, party. He even took the party up a notch by turning the water into wine. Sounds like, "ok, round of drinks on me for everyone." I know, I know, that's a bit much for some of you - I understand. I'm pushing the envelope here to make a point - Jesus was into entertainment. Let's take a look at another occasion - Mary and Martha were entertaining friends, family and guests. Well actually, Martha was doing all the entertaining. Mary was captivated by Jesus entertaining the people. The word entertainment in the Greek is the word "xenizo."

> ξενίζω **xĕnizō**, *xen-id´-zo;* from *3581;* to *be a host*, hospitality (pass. a *guest*); by impl. *be (make, appear) strange:—* entertain, lodge, (think it) strange.

This is why in Hebrews it says:

Hebrews 13:1 *Let brotherly love continue.* **2** *Do not forget to* **entertain** *strangers, for by so doing some have unwittingly entertained angels.*

Do not forget to entertain strangers. This means that at some point in our existence we had full knowledge that we were supposed to be hospitable and entertain even those we do not know very well. Paul said do not forget to entertain strangers right after he said let brotherly love continue. Entertain here is; "*philoxenia*," lit., "love of strangers" (*phileo*, "to love," and *xenos*, "a stranger or guest".)

Entertainment is an Expression of Love

My God, that is an awesome revelation. God gave us entertainment because he loves us. His form of entertainment allows us to drift off into the Heavenly Realm and not only forget the problems and things on our mind - but reprogram our minds to His thoughts which are higher! Now let's look deeper into the word philoxenia. This word "philoxenia" is translated hospitality. That is why 1 Peter 4:9 says to be hospitable to one another. I love it because he says be hospitable to one another but without grumbling. In other words, entertain each other without complaining. Invite people to your house, cook some good food and hang out.

***1 Peter 4:9** Be hospitable to one another without grumbling.*

We see this in the book of Acts. They broke bread from house to house and the church grew. The reason Peter said to do it without grumbling is because it takes a lot of work to prepare your house for others and to serve others. However, a major key is found here. When you entertain people you help divert their minds off of current problems and onto fellowship and communion. Think about it! You allow someone else to enter your course of love and service to break any thoughts from any problem they could be having. Praise God!

But wait......there's more!

God Had His People Entertain Those in the World

1 Samuel 16:16 *Let our lord now command thy servants, which are before thee, to seek out a man, who is a cunning player on an harp: and it shall come to pass, when the evil spirit from God is upon thee, that he shall play with his hand, and thou shalt be well.*

David entertained Saul and the Spirit of God was not with Saul. How much more should we who are anointed to play go into the world and play for those who need deliverance so it can be well with them? We must remember as the Church, that God is not afraid of sin or sinners. (I will cover the sin issue in the next chapter.) Jesus hung out with sinners to the point that he was accused of being one.

The Lord spoke to Cain in Genesis:

Genesis 4:6-7 *Then the Lord said to Cain, "Why are you angry? Why is your face downcast? If you do what is right, will you not be accepted? But if you do not do what is right, sin is crouching at your door; it desires to have you, but you must rule over it."*

We don't have to get all jacked up about sin, especially sin that belongs to someone else. If sin lies at the door, step over it. Take the gift you have (to act, sing, play an instrument, paint, whatever talent you have) and with the anointing of God, use it! Help someone like Saul experience the presence of God and get breakthrough or deliverance. Here is another one for you. They called Samson to play for the guests, to give sport. However you will see the joke was on them.

Judges 16:25-26 *So it happened, when their hearts were merry, that they said, "Call for Samson, that he may **perform** for us." So they called for Samson from the prison, and he performed for them. And they stationed him between the pillars. **26** Then Samson said to the lad who held him by the hand, "Let me feel the pillars which support the temple, so that I can lean on them."*

The word "perform" is the Hebrew word "sachaq," which is translated sport in the same verse in the King James Version (KJV.)

7832 שָׂחַק [*sachaq* /saw·**khak**/] v. A primitive root; TWOT 1905c; GK 8471; 36 occurrences; AV translates as "play" 10 times, "laugh" 10 times, "rejoice" three times, "scorn" three times, "sport" three times, "merry" twice, "mock" twice, "deride" once, "derision" once, and "mockers" once. **1** to laugh, play, mock. 1A (Qal). *1A1* to laugh (usually in contempt or derision). *1A2* to sport, play. 1B (Piel). *1B1* to make sport. *1B2* to jest. *1B3* to play (including instrumental music, singing, dancing).

Samson was called to perform for them – which in this case was to make a fool of him and laugh at him - for their entertainment. However, as I said before, the joke was on them. Samson killed everybody by pushing the pillars of the building until the whole building collapsed on them. The fact that sport and perform are used as a translation of the same word is no accident. The word sport (as in athletic) is a shortened version of the word "deport" or "disport," which means dis (away) + port (carry). So when we watch sports, our attention gets carried away by the diversion of the game at hand. This gift is amazing in God's Hand because we are allowed to see extraordinary people play by what is really the anointing of

God! We see them jump, hit, throw or run like Elijah did when God anointed him to outrun the chariot.

> **1 Kings 19:44-46** ...So he said, "Go up, say to Ahab,' Prepare your chariot, and go down before the rain stops you." ...So Ahab rode away and went to Jezreel. Then the hand of the Lord came upon Elijah and he girded up his loins and ran ahead of Ahab to the entrance of Jezreel.

More Scriptures Where the Word Sachaq is Used

> **1 Samuel 18:7** And the women answered one another as they **played,** and said, Saul hath slain his thousands, and David his ten thousands.

> **2 Samuel 2:14** And Abner said to Joab, Let the young men now arise, and **play** (compete NKJV) before us. And Joab said, Let them arise.

> **Psalm 2:2** The kings of the earth set themselves, And the rulers take counsel together, Against the LORD and against His Anointed, saying, **3** "Let us break Their bonds in pieces And cast away Their cords from us." **4** He who sits in the heavens shall **laugh;** The LORD shall hold them in derision.

> **2 Samuel 6:5** And David and all the House of Israel **played** before the LORD on all manner of instruments made of fir wood, even on harps, and on psalteries, and on timbrels, and on cornets, and on cymbals.

As we see in 2 Samuel 2:14, the young men were told to arise and play before them, which was to entertain Abner and those watching. In Psalms 2:4, the Lord laughs at the performance of kings and rulers who try to take counsel against him and his anointed. We should have no fear going into

Hurricane Entertainment (or as Lance Wallnau says, the Entertainment Mountain) to dispossess the kings of that mountain. God laughs when they try to form a strategy against us. Literally, when people come up against God and his anointed people, it is entertainment for him. Think about anyone or any demon coming against you and just laugh at that!

Let's Act Like the Man

God doesn't even mind if we play the role and become actors or actresses. After all, our life is the role of a lifetime; it's a movie God is producing. Paul said in Corinthians:

> *1 Corinthians 11:1 Follow me as I follow Christ.*

The Greek word follow is the word "mimeomai" where we get the word mime or actor.

We can see aspects of entertainment throughout the Word of God. Joab said to David's Mighty Men the following before going into battle against the Syrians:

> *2 Samuel 10:12 (KJV) Be of good courage, and let us **play the men** for our people, and for the cities of our God: and the LORD do that which seemeth him good.*

That's right, play the men. If you don't feel like a champion act like it till it is so. Play the man, act it out because you are in the role of a lifetime! You only get one take; there are no do-overs and the cameras are always rolling. Jesus has not only given you the script, He is the script-tures! Study your lines and don't worry about the bloopers. The Holy Spirit is the Director - He uses the bloopers to show people watching your life (a living epistle as in 2 Corinthians 3:3) that it's okay to make mistakes.

2 Corinthians 3:3 clearly *you are* an epistle of Christ, ministered by us, written not with ink but by the Spirit of the living God, not on tablets of stone but on tablets of flesh, *that is,* of the heart.

We have the Angelic Host as the supporting cast and because God is also the Executive Producer, the budget for this film is unlimited. There were no auditions for this film - as soon as you signed up as a Christian and became part of the Kingdom Union, you got the role. Ha Ha! This is too much fun! I could go on with that analogy but let's go to the next chapter. We are going to one of our primary locations for most of our Hurricane Entertainment scenes.

Notes

Chapter Four

The Lion's Den

NOW THAT WE HAVE LOOKED at the backdrop of Hurricane Entertainment, uncovered the enemy's plans and saw that *Entertainment is a God Eyedea* (and all over the Bible,) let's go if you will on the set of the Lion's Den better known as Hollywood. Even if you feel the title I've given it is true for now, when you look from the eye of our loving Father's redemptive plan, you can't help but see Hollywood differently. The truth is, God shut the mouth of that lion. At best, after we stand up to this imitation of a lion, we will watch it shake like the cowardly lion from the Wizard of Oz. Yes, I know that Hollywood, through Hurricane Entertainment, has taken some of our brightest childhood stars. It has turned them from innocent, cute kids into twerking machines. It has taken some of the church's greatest talents and caught them in a downward spiral of drugs, even unto death. At the same time, the truth is that this lion is powerless and looking for who he can devour. If we don't let him, he has no power to eat. I want to at least minimize (if not completely stop) the number of people lost in the Lion's Den pursuing a God given dream to entertain the world.

I believe it will help us if we look at the negative side of Hollywood for what it really is - a community full of starving artists. You're probably thinking, starving artist? What? The ones we are talking about are the very ones that are producing the entertainment, which means they are paid. You may be saying "yeah jo'EL, starving artists are those singers, songwriters, actors and actresses that haven't made it yet" (living in the very dance studio they are practicing in like Jennifer Lopez did.) You say "those are the ones working at odd jobs that they can easily quit when the right audition or opportunity blows their way." Starving artists are the ones making just barely enough to survive. My friends, looking on the surface I say you're absolutely right. However, the starving I'm talking about is the kind that causes people to look for love in all the wrong places. It's a starving that all the fame in the world can't satisfy. This is why you see those with money and fame commit suicide, have run-ins with the law or die from drug abuse or overdose.

The starving I'm talking about comes from a spiritual hunger for the love that only Papa God can quench. This problem is not just for those in Hollywood though, no way. This is a universal problem for sure. But for those creative people who grab our attention with God given gifts, the devil has targeted them and branded them as his. Let's walk closer to the eye of this storm as we look at the origin of Hollywood.

Hollywood Had a Humble Beginning

Hollywood or Hollywoodland, as the sign read in 1923 to advertise a new housing development, started off in 1853 with a single adobe hut on the land outside of Los Angeles. Growing crops was so successful there that by 1870 it became a thriving agricultural community. The first street in town was named Prospect Avenue (but was later changed to Hollywood Boulevard.)   In the early 1900's, filmmakers began moving to the Los Angeles area to avoid Thomas Edison's Motion Picture Patents Company located in New Jersey.

Edison owned most of the movie patents and would sue other filmmakers to stop their productions. In 1943, when the sign was in desperate need of repair, the Hollywood Chamber of Commerce was given authority to remove the last four letters and restore the remaining portions of the sign on the hillside. I would like to think they misinterpreted the letters God really wanted to remove so that it would read Holywood. Today, after hosting 20th Century Fox, MGM, Paramount and Warner Bros., Paramount is the last major movie studio still located there.

Family tradition says that Harvey and Ida Wilcox moved to California after the death of their 18 month old baby and consoled themselves by taking buggy rides to the beautiful canyons west of Los Angeles. Harvey ended up purchasing one of their favorite areas, full of fig and apricot orchards, for $150 per acre. After Harvey failed at growing fruit he decided to subdivide the land and sell the lots at $1,000 each. It was Ida Wilcox who renamed Prospect Avenue to Hollywoodland and called one of the new streets Sunset Boulevard in order to appeal to buyers. I don't believe that Ida named the street Sunset Boulevard just to appeal to buyers. I believe she had a vision of a place of beauty. I believe she saw beauty for the ashes of her baby that died. The Los Angeles Times Obituary stated that it was Daeida's dream of beauty that gave world fame to Hollywood years before the first movie company arrived in 1913. Daeida Hartell Wilcox Beveridge was inducted into the Ohio Women's Hall of Fame in 1995.

Could it be that a woman's desire for beauty to be birthed from her pain caused demonic spirits to bring women in Hollywood so much ugliness and pain - in the very same place God gave this woman so much purpose to create beauty? I don't know, but it seems very likely to me. The fact that filmmakers originally came to that land for freedom to create without manipulation and control by Edison to me has the fingerprint of Papa God. The filmmakers were so afraid of Edison that when agents from Edison's company came to find and stop them, they would escape quickly to Mexico. It sounds to me like the origin of Hollywood was a desire for freedom and beauty in a fruitful, agricultural land.

Handling Hollywood Today

Obviously, Hollywood is a lot different today than it was even in the golden age from 1927-1948. Hollywood (not necessarily the place but the icon) definitely is creating much of the climate producing the forceful winds of Hurricane Entertainment. We, as the body of Christ, need a strategy from Heaven to occupy the Mountain of Entertainment until Christ comes. The strategy is very simple and is God's Number One tactic to win a battle.

It's Love!

My friend, Shawn Bolz, often says that we cannot possess or have authority over what we do not love. If we are to possess Hollywood we have to love the people in it. The lions in the Lion's Den can't harm us if we move under the umbrella of love. As I'm writing I feel the need to point out and make clear who the lion imposter is, so there is no confusion or thinking that I'm talking about people. The Bible says the devil is **like** a roaring lion seeking whom he may devour; our fight is not against people. One of the main concepts we need to be aware of to calm this storm is that we do not wrestle against flesh and blood but against demonic spirits.

> ***Ephesians 6:12*** *For we wrestle not against flesh and blood, but against principalities, against powers, against the rulers of the darkness of this world, against spiritual wickedness in high places.*

I know I may be preaching to the choir but as senior leader of a church of about 200 members, I see it over and over again. We as people get offended and want to attack or attach the blame on a person. We see the sin of the person and want to stay far away from them out of anger, hurt, shock or fear we may be contaminated by their actions. Right here is where the rubber meets the road as far as I'm concerned. If we don't get this right the world will continue to be discipled by Hurricane Entertainment. It is shaping our culture, our fashion, our speech, the way we feel about our bodies and everything else in between. With being contaminated in mind and staying far away from sin, how do we handle scriptures like 2 Corinthians 6:14 that seem to agree?

> **2 Corinthians 6:14** *Do not be unequally yoked together with unbelievers. For what fellowship has righteousness with lawlessness? And what communion has light with darkness?*

After looking at that scripture you too may be thinking well then, how can we go into the world and make disciples if we are to come out from among them? My friends, that is a good question! I believe looking at this scripture the wrong way may explain why we have such a problem with Christians being involved in most forms of entertainment.

> **2 Corinthians 6:11** *O Corinthians! We have spoken openly to you, our heart is wide open.* **12** *You are not restricted by us, but you are restricted by your own affections.* **13** *Now in return for the same (I speak as to children), you also be open.* **14** *Do not be unequally yoked together with unbelievers. For what fellowship has righteousness with lawlessness? And what communion has light with darkness?* **15** *And what accord has Christ with Belial? Or what part has a believer with an unbeliever?* **16** *And what agreement has the temple of God with idols? For you are the temple of the living God. As God has said: "I will dwell in them And walk among them. I will be their God, And they shall be My people."* **17** *Therefore "Come out from among them And be separate, says the Lord. Do not touch what is unclean, And I will receive you."* **18** *"I will be a Father to you, And you shall be My sons and daughters, Says the LORD Almighty."*

> **2 Corinthians 7:1** *Therefore, having these promises, beloved, let us cleanse ourselves from all filthiness of the flesh and spirit, perfecting holiness in the fear of God.*

Paul was not simply telling them to stay away from sinners. He started by telling them that we are not restricting you. It is your own affections that cause you to be restricted from what I'm about to tell you to stay away from. Here is an example for you. If you have a drinking problem, you should stay away from drinking until you no longer have a desire or affection for alcohol. If you love to gamble, Las Vegas probably isn't the spot for you to go to. However, I hate gambling because I hate to lose money - whenever I go to Las Vegas I never have to worry about that problem. If you don't have an affection for pornography, you may be able to work with the people in that industry. You will not be affected by the temptation. Jesus said the devil has come to tempt me but has found nothing in me. When we have no root in us for satan to grab us with, the temptations will have no effect on us.

The word fellowship also means "intercourse." Paul is asking: why would you want to enter the course or direction of a nonbeliever when we should be leading them to a different course by leading them to the way? Jesus is the way - we should be leading people to his course. His course is the course which he prepared for them beforehand (Ephesians 2:10.)

> **Ephesians 2:10** *For we are Gods handiwork, created in Christ Jesus to do good works, which God prepared in advance for us to do.*

Earlier I was talking about the sin issue - let's dig into that for a minute. I want to point out to you that when Paul was saying be open, he was saying be enlarged. A better way of saying that is to let your heart be enlarged. God has called us to enlarge our territory but if our heart is closed, it's impossible.

Paul was telling them open your heart; just don't get entangled with the beliefs of an unbeliever or idol worshipper.

Sin is Not an Issue

I taught at my church, "The 10 Myths of Someone Else's Sin," which was enlightening to most people. As I said in Chapter 2 and is worth reiterating, God is not afraid of sin. God conquered sin and death, Hallelujah! The truth about sin is that Jesus took care of sin; his blood is the forgiveness of sin.

> *Ephesians 1:7 In Him we have redemption through His blood, the* **forgiveness** *of sins, according to the riches of His grace.*

I will cover in depth and teach what Jesus did on the cross for people in my upcoming book on identity, but let me say this in regard to that topic. All of our sins have been paid for. Your sins, my sins, our past, present and future sins - by the death, burial and resurrection of Jesus – all have been paid for. All we have to do is receive the gift of forgiveness for our sins, confess with our mouth that Jesus is Lord and believe it in our heart (Romans 10:9.)

> *Romans 10:9 If you declare with your mouth, "Jesus is Lord," and believe in your heart that God raised him from the dead, you will be saved.*

After Jesus paid the price for sin and poured his blood on the mercy seat, you don't need to ask for forgiveness for your sins because that is what his blood did. Jesus paid the price for sin so you only need to repent, which is to change your mind and go the other way. Whoa Nelly, look at that, repent means to change your mind. This is why satan wants to entertain you - to keep your mind captivated so that it doesn't change.

A lot of people are under the impression that we have to keep asking God to forgive us for our sins over and over - I guess there is no major harm in that action. However, you can ask for forgiveness over and over and never be required to change. Repentance requires you to change; it also places a demand on you to bear the fruit of repentance (Matthew 3:8).

Matthew 3:8 *Therefore bear fruits worthy of repentance,*

Praise God sin is not an issue. God does not want us to focus on sin; remember - whatever you focus on, meditate on or are entertained by will be exactly what you get. A major key to defeating a life of sin is not to focus on sin but to awake to righteousness (1 Corinthians 15:34).

1 Corinthians 15:34 *Awake to righteousness, and do not sin; for some do not have the knowledge of God. I speak this to your shame.*

The bottom line is: if you are an Entertainer and around nonbelievers, you will not be affected if you are not in communion with them. Now, before I explain why I'm saying this let me show you another scripture along the same lines to take care of all the questions that arise from misinterpreting the word. Let's look at 1 Corinthians 15:33 in three different translations.

1 Corinthians 15:33 (AV) *Be not deceived: evil communications corrupt good manners.*

1 Corinthians 15:33 (KJV) *Do not be deceived: "Evil company corrupts good habits."*

1 Corinthians 15:33 (NAB) *Do not be led astray: "Bad company corrupts good morals."*

Many times we are reading the right script but not interpreting it from the eyes of the one who wrote it. An actor can read the right lines all they want, but if they don't convey the heart of the writer the scene will come out wrong. With that thought in mind, let's look at what the writer was saying in the above scriptures. Communion, communications and company all point back to intimacy. As I pointed out earlier, Paul saying to be holy and come out from among them is not saying to avoid nonbelievers. He is saying that their beliefs should not become your beliefs. You see, you can be around people doing whatever they want if you are filling yourself with the Holy Spirit and letting God entertain you. As long as you don't get into a union with their thoughts, let their thoughts join yours or let their thoughts become yours, you'll be fine. So in terms of company, communication or communion - if you have not made their belief or nonbelief common with yours - or commune (intercourse) with yours by joining your beliefs with theirs - then you are not in communion. You are free to love them right out of darkness and into light, right out of pain and into peace, right out of an identity issue to the reality of being a son or daughter to a loving Father.

I know, I know, some of you think that innocent little Susie going into such a seductive filled environment would be a major problem. My friend, you may be right. Again, there is only a problem when a baby Christian (who is not yet ready for such an assignment) goes into such an environment unprepared. They aren't mature enough yet to be around nonbelievers in that capacity and they get pulled away from Christ. Since this is a problem for some and not for all; the restrictions should not apply to all who are called to be submerged in this culture and surrounded consistently by people who may not be on the same page spiritually. If innocent little Susie was properly prepared and full of the Holy Spirit she would be the worst enemy the devil has ever seen - the biggest blessing to everyone she comes across in Hollywood.

I also want to interject - if you are on the outside of the entertainment community and occasionally run across entertainers from time to time - walk in love as Christ did. If you feel the need to discuss entertainers who are featured in the latest tabloids or entertainment news whom you have never met, speak life over them. You may be the only light they get to see. Friends, our position in Christ does not give us the right to treat nonbelievers like they will always be nonbelievers or that they are the problem. The truth is, if I was treated before I got saved like I would always be unsaved and be stuck where I was at that time in my life - I would have never experienced the love of the Father to be where I am now. I would guess that most of you probably fall into the same category as I did and needed the mercy of God.

> *Matthew 18:23 Therefore the kingdom of heaven is like a certain king who wanted to settle accounts with his servants. 24 And when he had begun to settle accounts, one was brought to him who owed him ten thousand talents. 25 But as he was not able to pay, his master commanded that he be sold, with his wife and children and all that he had, and that payment be made. 26 The servant therefore fell down before him, saying, 'Master, have patience with me, and I will pay you all.' 27 Then the master of that servant was moved with compassion, released him, and forgave him the debt. 28 "But that servant went out and found one of his fellow servants who owed him a hundred denarii; and*

*he laid hands on him and took him by the throat, saying, 'Pay me what you owe!' **29** So his fellow servant fell down at his feet and begged him, saying, 'Have patience with me, and I will pay you all.' **30** And he would not, but went and threw him into prison till he should pay the debt. **31** So when his fellow servants saw what had been done, they were very grieved, and came and told their master all that had been done. **32** Then his master, after he had called him, said to him, 'You wicked servant! I forgave you all that debt because you begged me. **33** Should you not also have had compassion on your fellow servant, just as I had pity on you?' **34** And his master was angry, and delivered him to the torturers until he should pay all that was due to him. **35** "So My heavenly Father also will do to you if each of you, from his heart, does not forgive his brother his trespasses."*

My friends, if we start trying to eliminate the tares we may pull up some of the wheat in our haste to remain clean and holy. Bill Johnson says it this way when it comes to our desire to stay clean from the world: "In the Old Testament what you touched could make you unclean, i.e. touching someone with leprosy, but in the New Testament when Jesus touched the lepers they became clean." Think about how Jesus dealt with Peter.

*__John 21:15__ So when they had eaten breakfast, Jesus said to Simon Peter, "Simon, son of Jonah, do you love Me more than these?" He said to Him, "Yes, Lord; You know that I love You." He said to him, "Feed My lambs." **16** He said to him again a second time, "Simon, son of Jonah, do you love Me?" He said to Him, "Yes, Lord; You know that I love You." He said to him, "Tend My sheep." **17** He said to him the third time, "Simon, son of Jonah, do you love Me?" Peter was grieved because*

He said to him the third time, "Do you love Me?" And he said to Him, "Lord, You know all things; You know that I love You." Jesus said to him, "Feed My sheep.

From this example we see how to love people in the Entertainment Industry who love God but are not perfect, while God is working on their heart. Before this conversation with Peter, Jesus told Peter that he was a rock and that Jesus would build his Church on the revelation Peter received from God. Peter had just received direct revelation from God, confirmed by Jesus.

My God....you would have thought that after such an encounter Peter would be singing in the choir, never watching an R-rated movie and only hanging out with perfect Pastors. Well as we know, that didn't happen. We see that after Peter had the revelation of who Jesus is he still had work to do on his character. Peter still cussed, he cut off a soldier's ear and even denied Jesus. What was the response from Jesus? Peter do you love me? **Jesus asked Peter the question "do you love me?" to pull out the love that was in Peter's heart, not the lies that were in Peter's head.** Jesus was not offended by Peter when he messed up. He loved him through his process - to the point where Peter could stand (in the book of Acts) boldly and address a crowd who thought he was drunk. If Jesus would have cut Peter off when he cut off the soldier's ear, Peter never would have walked out all the miracles he accomplished or become an instrumental person in the advancement of the Kingdom after Jesus was resurrected.

I believe this is the model for how we are to treat people in the Entertainment Industry, even those caught up in Hurricane Entertainment. They may not have their feet on solid ground and they may not be standing upright (righteous.) As a matter of fact, they may even be parallel with their feet flying in the wind. If we look through a God Eyedea, God sees they are holding on to a light pole so they don't blow away. You may be the light pole they have a hold of as God continues to reposition their heart, like he did Peter's. Yep, they are cussing, violent and maybe, you say, by what they produce and how they entertain, they are denying Jesus. This may be true - just like it was true for Peter. Exactly as it was for him, Jesus is preparing them to be those who have been forgiven much. They will be those just like the woman washing his feet with her hair who loved much. Let's take a look at this passage of scripture with this particular woman who had been forgiven much.

> **Luke 7:36** *Then one of the Pharisees asked Him to eat with him. And He went to the Pharisee's house, and sat down to eat.* **37** *And behold, a woman in the city who was a sinner, when she knew that Jesus sat at the table in the Pharisee's house, brought an alabaster flask of fragrant oil,* **38** *and stood at His feet behind Him weeping; and she began to wash His feet with her tears, and wiped them with the hair of her head; and she kissed His feet and anointed them with the fragrant oil.* **39** *Now when the Pharisee who had invited Him saw this, he spoke to himself, saying, "This Man, if He were a prophet, would know who and what manner of woman this is who is touching Him, for she is a sinner."* **40** *And Jesus answered and said to him, "Simon, I have something to say to you." So he said, "Teacher, say it."* **41** *"There was a certain creditor who had two debtors. One owed five hundred denarii, and the other fifty.* **42** *And when they had nothing with which to repay, he freely forgave them both. Tell Me, therefore, which of them will love him more?"* **43** *Simon answered and said, "I suppose the one whom he forgave more." And He said to him,*

"You have rightly judged." **44** *Then He turned to the woman and said to Simon, "Do you see this woman? I entered your house; you gave Me no water for My feet, but she has washed My feet with her tears and wiped them with the hair of her head.* **45** *You gave Me no kiss, but this woman has not ceased to kiss My feet since the time I came in.* **46** *You did not anoint My head with oil, but this woman has anointed My feet with fragrant oil. 47* **Therefore I say to you, her sins, which are many, are forgiven, for she loved much.** *But to whom little is forgiven, the same loves little."*

Did you see that? This woman loved much because she was forgiven much. This woman, who was already at a place of being forgiven, was called a sinner by the Pharisee. Our greatest entertainers are forgiven and may not know it. This is amazing to me! Those we see in the videos and movies that many would have nothing to do with will be some of the greatest lovers of Christ ever seen. I know this to be true, because I was one of them. Praise God!

Now I know some of you are probably still thinking hey - this is good that we love people who have not made Jesus their Lord - or even those who love Jesus but are working it out - but participating in some of their entertainment is taking it too far. So the question is where do we draw the line? I'm glad you asked! I will give my thoughts on that question in the last chapter.

Notes

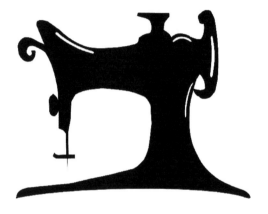

Chapter Five

What's Behind the Curtain?

INSTAGRAM POST @seejoel May, 2015
Behind every performance that entertains the audience there is a major production going on. The people are mostly unknown and although they work hard they remain behind the scenes. They make the movie, song, play, etc., run smooth and the entertainers look and sound good. This is a picture of the way many of us direct our lives. See my friends, the emotions in your subconscious mind control over 80% of what you do. What the audience gets to see comes from an assortment of thoughts in a cluster of emotions that are working hard to make you look good and sound good. However, for most people, just like the entertainers, it's only an act. If we pull back the curtain like in the Wizard

of Oz, we would see that the powerful person we thought was a Wiz is just a frail, harmless individual, subject to fear, stress, depression and pain just like everyone else. The question is, if we pulled back the curtains on your life and saw your real identity, what would we see? #entertainmentmountain #identity #emotions #playhard #lifestyle #results #kingdomCoaching #calling #identitycoaching #joEL #emm #entertainment #performance

Here, put on this travel suit. So you can fully understand where I'm at now and see behind the curtain of those who perform and entertain us who are not yet walking with God, I'm going to take you on a time travel trip back to the past. We land somewhere in 1975, because as far as I can remember, I've been in love with entertainment. I recall the trips our family took (driving for days) across the country from Oceanside, California to Albany or Augusta, Georgia. With nothing but time on our hands, my brother and I would pass the time by singing songs from our favorite television shows. Shows like Fat Albert, Good Times and The Jefferson's; even shows with songs and no words like "CHiPs" or The Streets of San Francisco." Well I know I'm dating myself now just a little bit, but hey, those were the good ole days.

My parents would have me come and dance for everyone during barbecues and when friends and family just got together to hang out. Yep, I grew up performing! I listened to music like Curtis Mayfield, B.T. Express, Earth, Wind and Fire - some of you know what I'm talking about. I'm telling you I loved the music of those days. But man, I can still feel the excitement I had when the first rap song I ever heard came out, called "Rappers Delight," by Sugarhill.

You remember…

I said a hip hop,
Hippie to the hippie,
The hip, hip a hop, and you don't stop, a rock it
To the bang bang boogie, say, up jump the boogie,
To the rhythm of the boogie, the beat.

Well that was it for me - I fell in love with making rhymes and poetry. In the fifth grade I filled our class book assignments with limericks. In between taking piano lessons and playing in both concert band and marching band, I excelled in rhymes. I followed rap all the way to high school, battling other hip hop artists in school. First I was beat boxing like the Fat Boys, then as a DJ I did school and house parties, even weddings. I will never forget spinning music at Dokie Williams's Wedding Reception. Dokie Williams was an Oceanside Boy who made it pro and played for the Oakland Raiders; so I was on Cloud Nine.

I began to get noticed as an MC, rapping at school in the hallways before class. I connected with Wilski, one of the dopest rappers at the school at the time; we formed the group B-Boy Rage. Our fame started to get out and helped us connect with James Wilson, one of the freshest DJ's at the time in North County San Diego. He was a few years older than us, which was cool because he had a good job and could afford the equipment we needed to start making our own songs. As a matter of fact he already had his own equipment; we were broke teenagers following a dream. You see it's like my friend, Lou Engle says – "God had a dream about you, then wrapped flesh around it so he can see it come to pass on the earth." When you get a dream from heaven that is a calling for your life it becomes a passion that is hard to shake. This is why you see sports players, whether they make it pro or not, go from playing the game to coaching the game. The calling is still burning!

To me, I was following a dream, but without Christ steering the ship, Hurricane Entertainment was blowing me into the wrong harbor. satan wanted us to work for him. On top of that, one thing you have to remember is that satan particularly loves music, as pipes and flutes were part of his body. Let's look at the revelation God gave the Prophet Ezekiel about how satan was made:

> **Ezekiel 28:13** *Thou hast been in Eden the garden of God; every precious stone was thy covering, the sardius, topaz, and the diamond, the beryl, the onyx, and the jasper, the sapphire, the emerald, and the carbuncle, and gold:* **the workmanship of thy tabrets and of thy pipes was prepared in thee in the day that thou wast created.**

Tabrets are similar to a modern day tambourine. satan also had pipes inside him. Before he sinned, I believe when he opened his mouth to speak, songs came out. Can you imagine what it must have been like to hear the glorious praise and worship that came from him when he just moved? Without Christ we are no match for the demonic spiritual realm. We finished our own demo tape (yep – tape) and it had a pretty catchy song on it called "More Bounce to the 40ty Ounce." This song had a sample from the break in James Brown's Song "I feel good." We took it to a guy we thought was a friend, called Trick. My God! We should have known what we were in for with a name like Trick.

Trick had some L.A. connections and before I knew it, we were in the backyard playing with Kurtis Blow. What!!!!! Are you kidding me - Rap Icon Kurtis Blow who rapped on the songs The Breaks, If I Ruled the World and Basketball? When the road to stardom shows up it tugs on the vision you have in your heart that is connected to heaven. This makes it hard to discern that you're going down the wrong path because everything in you is saying you're on the path of destiny. Remember, you are looking behind the curtain at artists who have been sacrificing for years, hoping this dream becomes a reality - with little or no filters or tools to fight the feelings of success beginning to bubble up.

The Kurtis Blow connection somehow led us to Lonzo from the World Class Wreckin Cru. It's very interesting how even when you are on the wrong road how many times you cross over the right one! We ended up making "More Bounce to The 40ty Ounce" a 12 inch record. It wasn't until many years later that we found out Trick took all the money we made from that record. Show Biz is brutal and no place for the weak at heart, it will eat you up and spit you out.

Well that was a lesson learned, but for us at the time, not knowing we were getting beat was a stepping stone to what was in our heart. We were starting to meet people like Dr. Dre - like I said, the wrong roads will cross the right roads. Later, we ended up with Eazy E, who was in the group NWA with Dr. Dre. Wow! As I look back, God was with me the whole time! This is why I say we can't count anyone out because our Father is working on them to come home all the time. All He needs us to know is that the coals are really diamonds going through the process.

What a time we were having! Wilski and I, along with Ghost and No Cents were now doing shows in clubs. Ha Ha! I recall being picked up in a limo and taken to the club we were performing at - only to get there and only have one mic! So we had to share one mic with rhymes that went back and forth like Run DMC. Too much fun; but that was part of paying your dues. Hurricane Entertainment makes you pay dues; then if you never find out a loving God has already paid the price for your sins you pay the price for sin. However, who can tell you you're being blown the wrong way when you're having the most fun in your life?

We began to occupy one of North County's Premier Young Adult Clubs called Distillery and with the help of Trick, brought in acts like Ice T., King T. and Bud from Love and Marriage. We brought in Young MC who had the hit song "Bust A Move." Things were going absolutely bananas. Girls were coming up to me just to rub on my head and kiss me. What more can a young man want? Listen close: God said that he would bless us and make our name great. The Bible says that the fame of Jesus spread. You see, we were created to be great and have fame so when we look at what Hurricane Entertainment has to offer, the lights begin to look real attractive. Things on the outside were going great. Things on the inside, behind the curtain, were experiencing shipwreck.

The accomplishment of a dream without the dream maker does nothing but leave a bigger unfulfilled hole in your heart. The more you are living the dream the more you see it's not filling the emptiness inside. Without the love of a Father who can remove the orphan spirit from our souls (so we can truly be connected to something bigger than us) we are tossed to and fro by the winds of Hurricane Entertainment.

Disaster struck as Wil and Ghost both went to jail at separate times. Wil got life for his third strike and Ghost got three years. No Cents and I found our way back to the drawing board without James Wilson (the DJ,) Wil (the other lead vocalist) and Ghost (who coproduced the music.) At the same time this was happening, the son I had right out of high school was caught in a custody battle between his mother and I; things were more than difficult. I will save that story for another book. Hurricane Entertainment will suck you into the promise of fame and fortune. It will make you choose between your family, friends and loved ones with the lie that what you're doing is for your family, friends and loved ones. What a trap!

I want to point out here that those called to the Entertainment Mountain caught up in Hurricane Entertainment are not following their idea; they are following God's Eyedea. This is why it's so hard to stop. Truth is they are not supposed to stop, just be redirected. Well, we were redirected all right but again not in the right direction. After going back to the drawing board, without skipping a beat, we began to make music in L.A. with No Cents (who during the time of our B-Boy Rage days began to get his own equipment.) We formed another group called Da I.B.S. and went to work.

Da I.B.S. started making music, networking and over time got connected to Julio G from the Mix Master. Julio G knew and was doing business with Eazy E. No Cents was doing business with Julio G. So as their paths continued to cross Eazy E started doing business with No Cents. While No Cents was networking and making beats out of this world, we added another member to Da I.B.S. named Lil Slim. Ghost introduced us by word of mouth but he went to jail before we could all connect. But as destiny would have it, I found him in the park one day. The day we met there was a DJ in the park. We hung out - he was rapping then I went in and kicked some rhymes - we went back and forth until we both had mutual respect for each other's skill. Soon after that we became a tight knit group and started to really pump out great music - people began to enjoy it and ask for more. As I'm telling you this hopefully you can see how deep the roots of sacrificing, dreaming and working hard to make it in show biz go before entertainers hit mainstream.

By the time we see people operating in their gifts and becoming famous, Hurricane Entertainment has blown and blown and blown (for some of them blown their minds) to a place of destruction. For Da I.B.S., our minds had definitely been blown into a dangerous place of giving everything we had to make it. We were oh so close to the dream becoming a reality with the World Class Wreckin Cru. Now we were even closer - with Eazy E, performing again in clubs, having a blast. This time with Eazy, Cocaine and Dru Down, all of them had hits out at the time - the venues were turned up a couple notches. Having a blast on the outside was awesome but again, on the inside I was just trying to hang on. Check out the first verse of the song I wrote titled "Jus Tryin to Hang On:"

I'm just trying to hang on a 40ty and two steps from a wino,

A year after Nine 4, what a mess stress is making my mind go,

Crazy as I live day by day it's pathetic,

Too many bills and $%@* up credit.

Feeling the worst, the first is my family's meal ticket,

I need to find a job but I mob and still kick it.

Wicked, is how I live as I,

See convenient stores but restrict from doing a lick as I pass by.

Cuz my homeboy Ghost from jail, he keeps me on the right trail,

Sending me letters and flicks in the mail.

Keepin me pumped so him no cents and slim,

And I can have a house one day with a pool ta swim.

But I'm grim, tryin to put food on the table,

Hearing my girl groan about the phone, and now they cut the cable

I'm able to make rent barely,

*Seein moms in the hospital $%!?#$*being hard that $%!?#$*scared me.*

Got me thinking of my own children, now left alone whealin

And dealin cuz I was never home chillen.

Then, as I sip gin for my troubles

Other Couples talk to my girlfriend bout the time they spend,

And the rhymes I send ain't producing

Riches, so my bitch just feels its no use in

Rapping, so I feel like busting a cap n $%!?#$ scrappin*

Always at a spot something happens

Is playing out, but staying out late on the block,

It's the $%!?#$ just murda with the 380 cocked.*

Leaving my girl to shed a tear, sayin I'm never here,

Its clear, we won't last another year.

Unless I bust through the doors of fame and my rhymes bang on,

I'm jus tryin to hang on.

Wow! When I wrote this song and it hit the streets I literally had people call me to ask if I was okay. I would have said no, I'm not okay, but that would have showed weakness - that was not acceptable. By now we were reaching what was to be the height of our career. We had started to travel with Easy E and Bone Thugs-N-Harmony. At that time, rap was everything to me. I had sacrificed almost everything to make it to where I was. We had been on 92.3 The Beat, the No. 1 Radio Station on the West Coast. We had not only been interviewed by Eazy E but had our music played as well. We got to freestyle on the air and everyone was feeling us. We were negotiating contracts to be signed to Ruthless Records. Eazy E had put us in *Rap Pages Magazine* as one of his groups coming out soon. Everything was looking like Hurricane Entertainment had blown a pathway for us and we were following the course.

Can you see how misled people can get when their heart's desire gets tangled up like barbwire with a false sense of accomplishment from Hurricane Entertainment? We were the Heroes of Oceanside - the first to really make it in the rap game. The first time I heard my song on the radio I was in L.A.; we were chilling with some girls and I felt like I had finally done it! All of Los Angeles that was tuned into The Beat was hearing what I wrote. How could that be wrong? Well, that wasn't wrong. What was wrong was that there was still a void in my soul that a moment even that outstanding could not fill. If we are going to reach those who are hurting in Hurricane Entertainment, we have to realize that on the outside they may have super power but on the inside they are frail, wounded people looking for help. Remember that in the next chapter as we star gaze at what's in front of the curtain.

Notes

Chapter Six

What's in Front of the Curtain?

INSTAGRAM POST @ seejoel May, 2015

Are you facing fear of the future, anxiety and worry or great expectations, hope and certainty? If what is behind the curtain is an unlocked identity which produces purpose, passion and progress then what is in front of the curtain will be remarkable. The world will be your audience waiting for you to deliver in the role of lifetime. You won't procrastinate because you understand in this role there is only one take and the cameras are always rolling. When your identity is unlocked and you perform for an audience of one the applause is continual! You can't help but elevate to the next level because the heart of an unlocked identity is always yelling "Encore! Encore!" What's in front of your curtain? #entertainmentmountain

I want to share with you what happened to me on what I call the "Front of the Curtain." We talked about what happened Behind the Curtain. Behind the Curtain (like most entertainers without Christ) I had wounds that had not been healed. There was a void I couldn't fill, there was purpose and identity that I couldn't find. My friends, no matter how much money they make or how much attention they get, they look for identity with the people they sleep with, the cars they drive, the houses they live in - and have no luck doing so. The drugs they take do not help and people on the outside continue to pull on them and put them on a pedestal. They are trying to find somewhere safe to hide or actually share with someone who they really are. They grew up chasing God's Eyedea, got pulled into Hurricane Entertainment and got swept away by the winds.

Everything for us was coming to a peak in 1994 when the unthinkable happened. We were in Cleveland, Ohio - home of Bone Thugs-N-Harmony - and they had already blown up. We had earned the right to open for them by smashing our other performances and moving ahead of others who were on the ticket. This was the biggest performance of my life. I remember taking the red eye flight from L.A. and shooting craps in the airport before leaving. I think No Cents got Eazy for a couple thousand! As we were waiting we ran into Hip Hop Artist Pete Rock and CL Smooth from the East Coast. I was living the dream - it couldn't get too much better than this. The life of a Hip Hop Star was in the works.

Now I had flown before but No Cents and T Spoon (who we took with us for extra support) had not. So when we got on the plane they started drinking shots. Ha Ha - we ended up wrestling on the plane - which nowadays would never be allowed to happen. Hopping from seat to seat, we were enjoying ourselves to the fullest! This is what God had always intended for us to have - a life full of enjoyment! The Bible says in John 10:10 that he came to give us life and that life more abundantly. A life full of joy!

> **John 10:10** *"The thief does not come except to steal, and to kill, and to destroy. I have come that they may have life, and that they may have it more abundantly.*

If I only knew then what I know now - I would have done things a lot differently! If I could have known what I know now when I was young and first hearing Rappers Delight - I wonder where I would be today? My friends, the best strategy for helping people in the Entertainment Mountain is to catch them when they are young - before they get caught up in Hurricane Entertainment. See, people who grow up in places where there are hurricanes year after year are taught when they are young what to do. Later in life when one comes, they know exactly what to do.

Knowing exactly what to do wasn't the case for us - we were headed for the biggest shock of our life and, as I said earlier, the unthinkable. Out in Ohio (after traveling most of the night and getting to bed around 2 or 3 in the morning) Eazy gives us a call to see if we wanted to go to the mall. Well we were too sleepy and declined; we told him we would be ready for mic checks later on. When that time came we loaded on the bus with Bone Thugs-N-Harmony and the rest of the performers and headed to the location of the show. Looking at Cleveland from the bus window and listening to Eazy and some of Bone talking about each other was amusing. Yes, I was being entertained. My mind was being taken off the nervous thought that there would be thousands of people at our show later on.

We pulled up to the lot where the show was to be held and did our mic checks without a problem. Later when we returned for the night to perform you could feel the electricity in the air. Of course we were still trying to work out and perfect what we were going to do. Earlier we had thrown out Zig Zag papers during our song Pass the Zig Zags. Eazy E loved that song (for obvious reasons) and it was to be the last song of our set. So now, with the show coming up we needed to find a store to get some Zig Zag papers. No Cents and I took off - not knowing where we were going. But we had a mindset to make it happen that had taken us this far - we weren't going to settle for less than that now. As I'm thinking back, we didn't have the slightest clue to what type of neighborhood we were in – we were just following the Yellow Brick Road of our Dreams to our Oz of Success.

As we walked up to the store we saw groups of dudes standing around looking at us. Maybe it was the fact we were dressed so fresh and so clean, ready for the performance or maybe they recognized that we weren't from their hood. Whatever the reason (we didn't stick around to find out) we got the Zig Zags we needed from the store and went back in a hurry. I mean we cleared them out of Zig Zags! See, you have to picture this - we were going to throw them into the audience and we couldn't just throw out one or two. We had to throw out handfuls of them! Ha Ha! Can you see the two of us walking back to the show with bags full of Zig Zags?

Now this chapter and the last chapter may not completely make sense to you as to why I put them in the book. I'm trying to connect the dots of Chapters 1 and 2 and show you the mindset and struggle of Entertainers, ordinary people who were apprehended by a God Eyedea. People like you and me who discovered they had passion for drawing or writing stories or taking pictures or kicking a ball or catching fish or running. They followed that passion and developed it into a talent that others would pay for to see or hear. They are ordinary people who, if fortunate enough, would do extraordinary things - all because God gave them a gift to entertain.

My friends, the gift of entertainment goes hand in hand with the ability to create and the one thing satan is not is a creator. Those who create heart pumping movies, songs that make us cry or paint beautiful pictures tap into the mind of God to pull on the creative force necessary to turn a blank canvas into something for the world to enjoy. The people in Hollywood or Broadway - from the walkways of Paris to the casinos of Las Vegas - were created to be conduits of Heaven. They were created to tell and show the grandeur of the Kingdom - no different than **Aimee Semple McPherson -** who preached with theatrics and used radio to broadcast the message of the Gospel. Everything we see in entertainment that is bad is a twisted version of something Papa God created to be good - even rap (which I will show you in a bit.) But let's go back to Cleveland to finish the show.

We were up next - it would have been nice if the person before us had the crowd hyped and ready for us to come out. On the contrary - they made the crowd hyped alright – they were in a frenzy - booing and throwing stuff on stage. The place that looked like the Apollo Theater turned into a mad house. Dru Down (who we later started calling Boo Down) was forced off the stage and ended his set abruptly. The crowd did not care for the negative references to woman being delivered with little or no lyrical skills. That which the Bay Area of Oakland loved (a dope beat, a cool voice and someone who could rhyme) was not cutting it in Cleveland.

Imagine what happens to an image made of glass that is only as good as the fans that sing its praise at the time. The roller coaster ride of being up one minute and down the next minute - so far down that only suicide makes sense. How do you think they feel - being subject to abuse from fans that were with them as long as they produced - but are now making fun of them - like a boxer who was the champ and now the chump? How do you think they feel - when they receive tongue lashings on all sides from the world - then Christians who are supposed to know what love is, talk bad about them also?

Well, we were in that type of environment and now taking the stage. Clear as a bell I can still see the trash hitting us when we first started rapping and one of my first lines said bitch. Excuse me for the language but feel me. We were now getting booed but going on with the show. Thank God we had great skills and lyrics that were able to calm the spirit of anger (like David who played and calmed the spirits troubling Saul.) By the end of that song we had the crowd singing the hook to our song "My Ho" - the crowd was totally with us by the time we got to our last song "Pass the Zig Zags." Eazy was so happy we saved the show he came on stage with a big blunt full of weed to pass around to us. As we rapped and threw out the Zig Zags it was like time went into slow motion - all the sound around me was muted as I savored the moment. It was surreal.

What a remarkable time we had! The plane ride home had nothing but hopes for the future that was looking bright - only to run into the unthinkable when we got home. We went into the studio to finish the CD to be released on Ruthless Records. We finished negotiating a healthy contract using lawyers who worked for the group "The Whispers." Oh yeah, we learned from Trick - we weren't going to get burned twice. As we were putting the finishing bow on everything, I got a call from No Cents saying he was hearing rumors that Eazy was in the hospital with AIDS. Oh Lord, no better than that - as some of my church mothers would say - Oh Lawd, this can't be true.

Eazy connected with No Cents and told him a direct line Straight Outta the movie Straight Outta Compton. Exactly what was said to Dr. Dre as he walked out of the hospital room is what he said to No Cents: "Don't worry bout nothin, I'll be out in no time." Eazy never made it out of the hospital room. By then we had heard the confirming words on MTV that Eric Wright indeed had aids; shortly after that we received the news that he passed away. My heart melted as my mind went back to a scene in Cleveland - we were going up to our room for the night to go sleep - Bone and Eazy were going to their rooms to party. I vividly see the gorgeous young lady who stepped into the elevator on her way to mostly likely sleep with a rap star that she had no idea had AIDS. Hurricane Entertainment was moving at top speed, blowing death and killing innocent people not prepared for the storm.

This was a wakeup call - but not quite enough yet to make me come from Behind the Curtain to live in Front of the Curtain. We regrouped (as we always did) and connected with Julio G, who took over the show Eazy E had on 92.3, "The Beat." It was on Saturday night and Eazy called it "The Ruthless Radio Show." Julio G took over and never looked back - he shortly became the radio host for The Beat from 6-10pm, Monday through Friday. First we made a song for him for the 9 O'clock Bomb - which was an hour of mixing nothing but hip hop at 9pm. Soon after that we did an opening song for him and people loved it. It was kind of eerie that Julio, on one of the days he premiered our song "Jus Tryin to Hang On," said "These are my homeboys Da I.B.S., they do my intros and they will be doing them till I'm out." Well, right after, he had another rapper do his intro and wouldn't you know, he was out. The Beat replaced him with another host. Wow! There is more power in our words than we can imagine. Well, we were doing his intro song and had music on The Beat for months (almost a whole year) and in the middle of that, something happened to me. I was getting tired of the winds of Hurricane Entertainment. I was feeling like what would seem to be a picture of someone deeply leaning forward - trying to walk against the wind - but not going anywhere. My mother was praying for me (as I was coming home from partying she was already up for the day praying.) My mother's prayers were literally tormenting the demons trying to kill my purpose to entertain people the way God had the Eyedea for me to do. It was like life meeting death when I got home, like Jesus in the Book of Luke.

Luke 7:11-15 *Now it happened, the day after, that He went into a city called Nain and many of His disciples went with Him, and a large crowd. And when He came near the gate of the city, behold, a dead man was being carried out, the only son of his mother and she was a widow. And a large crowd from the city was with her. When the Lord saw her, He had compassion on her and said to her, "Do not weep." Then He came and touched the open coffin, and those who carried him stood still. And He said, "Young man, I say to you, 'arise.'" So he who was dead sat up and began to speak. And He presented him to his mother.*

Jesus was walking down the street, crossing paths with a funeral procession carrying the son of a widow woman - who was laid out in a coffin. Just like when Jesus touched him and he got up, the Holy Spirit touched me and BAM, I got up!

Immediately I could see! I could see how to write fresh rhymes that gave God Glory that I could not do before. Every attempt I had made before was futile - the songs or lyrics were so wack. For those of you who don't understand street lingo, wack means the songs and lyrics were terrible. I was certain that writing Christian raps was not for me so I got discouraged and stopped trying. The problem was, I was trying to tap into something that had Spiritual Boundaries. Look at what the scriptures say:

1 Corinthians 2:14 *But the natural man does not receive the things of the Spirit of God, for they are foolishness to him; nor can he know them, because they are spiritually discerned.*

This is a huge point we have to take into consideration. Sometimes we are trying to get unsaved entertainers to discern things that they cannot discern. We want them to see what we see and get upset that they don't. This is why love is so important! Love is a tangible representation of God in Spirit that they can't see. The first thing we need to do for them is to pray (like my mother prayed for me.) This is where the battle is won or lost. In the middle of the storm referred to in Chapter 4, I believe Jesus was talking through dreams with the Father. We have to tap into the Spirit for what God sees for the Entertainment Industry and the Entertainers in it.

Well as time went on (after I got up out of the coffin of blindness and sin,) we were still on 92.3 doing the opening songs for Julio G - and nothing lacked. The people had no idea I went from Behind the Curtain to in Front of the Curtain, in other words unsaved to saved. You see, songs with cussing were not allowed on the radio at that time. The theme was no color lines and increase the peace. No cussing and a theme of peace made it difficult for people to tell that I had got saved when they heard the radio drops. Rapping and being able to do it for God was awesome! Praise God that *Entertainment is a God Eyedea* and right up my alley. I went on to open for KRS One - not as a secular rapper but as a Christian Rapper - and not in a church. I opened up for KRS One at the famous House of Blues in L.A.

Again, God was pointing me to the fact that for me to be in Entertainment was His Eyedea. If you walk in his wisdom you can position yourself right in the middle of it - in all of its secular fullness - and still accomplish what is the will of the Lord! As I was ending phase one of my rap career I was performing in and out of the church - entertaining people like the late great Bishop Veron Ashe to hip hop heads like Mad Lion. My time digging in the word was amazing, full of revelation after Revelayshn. As I said earlier, I even found out that rapping was in the Bible, so let's look at it now.

First, let me point out that I said Rap was in the Bible not rhyming. Rhyming is the syncopated connection of like sounding words creating harmony and unity in the thought process of the listener. Rhymes are words in harmony. Second, Rap is a form of poetry and poetry is all throughout the Bible. Psalms 119 is notable for its acrostic poetry. In Psalms 119 the first letter of each Stanza is a letter of the Hebrew Alphabet. Third, Rap is poetry put to a beat or music. Rap is synchronized preaching. The power of music and preaching combined. Rap is rhythmic sounds like waves or a heartbeat or breathing. When the rhythm is seamless it flows - which is why Rap is referred to as a flow.

Let's go further from the basic standpoint that God is the source of all things created. This point is key to understanding that Rap is in the Bible. Here is what the Bible says in Colossians:

> **Colossians 1:16** *For by Him all things were created that are in heaven and that are on earth, visible and invisible, whether thrones or dominions or principalities or powers. All things were created through Him and for Him. **17**And He is before all things, and in Him all things consist.*

The first Rap was in the Bible, it was the first song recorded in the Bible. They sang a song - but they spoke it. In Exodus, the Bible says Israel sang a song but that they spoke the song.

> **Exodus 15:1** *Then Moses and the children of Israel sang this song to the Lord, and **spoke**, saying: "I will sing to the Lord,*

For He has triumphed gloriously! The horse and its rider He has thrown into the sea!"

The word used here for spoke is the word "amar:"

amar (אָמַר, 559), "to say, speak, tell, command, answer."
Spoke =âmar, *aw-mar';* a prim. root; to *say* (used with great latitude):— answer, appoint, avouch, bid, boast self, call, certify, challenge, charge, + (at the, give) command (-ment), commune, consider, declare, demand, × desire, determine, × expressly, × indeed, × intend, name, × plainly, promise, publish, report, require, say, speak (against, of), × still, × suppose, talk, tell, term, × that is, × think, use [speech], utter, × verily, × yet.

This is the same word used in Genesis:

Genesis 1:3 *Then God said (amar) "Let there be light"; and there was light.*

In Exodus 15:1 when the children sang the song they really spoke it! When you speak a song you are speaking in a poetic flow. What's interesting is that many rappers express themselves in many of the words that are described in the Hebrew word amar. They boast self, challenge, report, some even certify they are the best lol. Here is another example from when God told Moses to speak in the ears of the people.

Deuteronomy 31:19 *"Now therefore, write down this song for yourselves, and teach it to the children of Israel; put it in their mouths, that this song may be a witness for Me against the children of Israel."*

Deuteronomy 32:44 *So Moses came with Joshua the son of Nun and* **spoke** *all the words of this song in the hearing of the people.*

Okay one more, but let's look at the New Testament!

Ephesians 5:19…speaking *to one another in psalms and hymns and spiritual songs, singing and making melody in your heart to the Lord.*

Just like in the Old Testament, the word speaking means speaking. Funny huh!

2980. λαλέω **laléō,** *lal-eh´-o;* a prol. form of an otherwise obs. verb; to *talk,* i.e. *utter* words:— preach, say, speak (after), talk, tell, utter.

Here is one of many scriptures the word laleo is used in;

Matthew 10:19 *But when they deliver you up, do not worry about how or what you should* **speak.** *For it will be given to you in that hour what you should* **speak.**

I believe when they were speaking songs they were rapping - speaking in a rhythmic flow that made it a song - the power of preaching and song at its best. There are many other examples in the Bible of singing songs and speaking songs, but I will let you have the fun of discovering them for yourself. So let's go back to the story.

By now, with revelation flowing from the Word of God, having cracked the code to writing good Christian lyrics, I was ready for the next stage. I was ready for where God told me during prayer he would send me - walking in the light - going into Hollywood like the Trojan Horse. In this last chapter I will show you a glimpse of what has been happening as I continue to walk in the light. As a matter of fact: In the Lights! Camera! Action!

Notes

Chapter Seven

Lights! Camera! Action!

I was recently in a movie called "G7," produced by and starring Snoop Dogg. The movie was masterfully written and directed by Dah Dah, a longtime friend of mine. G7 has a good message to it but the content is about as street as it gets. In the movie I play the Pastor that preached at the funeral! I also had some one-on-one scenes with Tyrin Turner - better known as Caine - who played a brilliant roll in Menace to Society. During the film I got to preach; I was told to freestyle my lines like I was at church preaching! We did about five takes to get different camera shots. In between each

111

take I preached a different sermon – the whole time there was weed smoke in the air (I think I got a bit of a contact high lol!) At the same time darkness was prevalent the light was shining and God was moving!

After I finished preaching during one of the takes, one of the guys said: "man you memorized all that?" The place erupted with laughter - Dah Dah said, "naw man he's a real Pastor." I told him "this is what's in my heart" and he shook his head, very impressed. I believe a seed was planted in his heart. Now moving on, if you know anything about filming you know it was a long day with a lot of standing around - I entertained myself and others by making beats on the pulpit. Most of the people there joined in - either singing or dancing or laughing and smiling. Think about that for a moment. Their idea of God may have changed from a stuffy old man upstairs to a fun loving papa who likes to enjoy life! Anyway, as I was beating on the pulpit the cast of the movie danced and had a good time.

As I said before in so many words, entertaining people is in me. God made me that way! In between filming G7, I was able to hold the people's attention and divert their mind away from the boredom of standing around waiting for the cameramen to get into position and get the right lighting etc. The Holy Spirit positioned me in a place to entertain the people there and because of the messages I was preaching, God was getting the Glory! One time when I was preaching and just for fun I said 'life isn't a game, you better check yo self be 4 u wreck yo self' - this was a quote from Ice Cube's song titled the same! Immediately Snoop and everyone in the building burst out laughing again. What happened? I believe I caused joy to enter a room that before was seriously quiet.

The next scene I had God opened the door for me to give a prophetic word to one of the main actors. This prophetic word was so right on that the person I gave it to wanted to exchange numbers; we still connect to this day. I could see that person's soul, thirsty for a good word, become refreshed with what our Papa had to say through the Holy Spirit. Others came up to me afterwards and started talking about how they were trying to get it right etc. (probably from the conviction of the word from when I was preaching in-between takes.) What was awesome was that I didn't preach that anyone there was a sinner or some bad person. I preached once on the Love of God, once about the Kingdom, once about his Word and I don't remember the rest. But as you can see, if we just let our light shine the gentiles will run to it.

> *Isaiah 60:1 Arise, shine; For your light has come! And the glory of the LORD is risen upon you. 2 For behold, the darkness shall cover the earth, And deep darkness the people; But the LORD will arise over you, And His glory will be seen upon you. 3 The Gentiles shall come to your light, And kings to the brightness of your rising. 4 "Lift up your eyes all around, and see: They all gather together, they come to you; Your sons shall come from afar, And your daughters shall be nursed at your side. 5 Then you shall see and become radiant, And your heart shall swell with joy; Because the abundance of the sea shall be turned to you, The wealth of the Gentiles shall come to you.*

If we just let our light shine, have confidence in the Holy Spirit, be ready and obedient to say and do what he asks us to do instantly, in season and out, we will see much better results! When we talk to people in the Entertainment Industry and show them the gold that is in them instead of what we think is their trash, they will run to our light. As Christians we don't have to be worried about interacting with people in the world who may be having temporary issues. Jesus said be of good cheer, I have overcome the world.

> **John 16:33** *"These things I have spoken to you, that in Me you may have peace. In the world you will have tribulation but be of good cheer, I have overcome the world."*

Although Jesus had no problem being around people who needed the love of God, the religious people back then did and still do today. Let's look at the response of the religious folk in those days regarding the interaction Jesus had with who the Pharisees called a sinner.

> **Luke 7:39** *Now when the Pharisee who had invited Him saw this, he spoke to himself, saying, "This Man, if He were a prophet, would know who and what manner of woman this is who is touching Him, for she is a sinner."*

Jesus responded to the religious people this way, take a look:

> **Matthew 9:10** *Now it happened, as Jesus sat at the table in the house, that behold, many tax collectors and sinners came and sat down with Him and His disciples.* **11** *And when the Pharisees saw it, they said to His disciples, "Why does your Teacher eat with tax collectors and sinners?"* **12** *When Jesus heard that, He said to them, "Those who are well have no need of a physician, but those who are sick."*

Jehovah Rophe lives in us; so if we don't go how is he going to go and bring the healing we say we want the lost to experience? When we go into the world, where do we draw the line with what we will do, watch, endorse and be a part of? These are questions we desperately need answers to! We need the Wisdom of God and the help of the Holy Spirit to rightly discern. I'm going to show you some things I learned through prayer, study, walking it out and talking to others with a similar call to the Entertainment Industry. So let me address the question.

The Line is drawn by Purpose

I believe when we go into darkness, especially the one caused by Hurricane Entertainment, it needs to be because of assignment and purpose. Take a look at what Jesus said getting ready to preach to the lost sheep of Israel. Specifically, Jesus preached to the lost sheep of Israel who were sinners, the ones the religious people looked down on (like the tax collectors, prostitutes, publicans, etc.)

> **Mark 1:36** *And Simon and those who were with Him searched for Him.* **37***When they found Him, they said to Him,* **"Everyone is looking for You."** **38***But He said to them, "Let us go into the next towns that I may preach there also, because for this* **purpose** *I have come forth."*

Notice that everyone was looking for Jesus but Jesus went into those places because of purpose. Jesus did not go to them because he had affections for the things they were doing. For instance; if you're in a club, at a party, acting in a movie, singing on a CD, on a sports team or painting a picture, what is the Kingdom Purpose? Who sent you? Jesus went where he was sent. Here is another good question: What is the wisdom that you are operating in? Remember, wisdom is justified by her children. This means there should be fruit from what God is telling you to do that brings Glory to Him and advances the Kingdom. Also, who are you accountable to or partnered up with?

Seeking the Lord on the issue of where do we draw the line - I felt like the instructions of the Holy Spirt were this: if you are going to be involved in a movie or song etc. there are a couple of ways to go about it.

1. **If you're going to be in a dark movie or on a dark song or project, be the light and the salt**.

Play a good character or make your lyrics represent the King of Kings and give him Glory. God will draw attention to the light that you represent.

2. **You can play a bad character or role in a good movie.**

The Bible is full of evil characters in a good book. If we were to act out the Bible, someone would have to play the bad guys.

I believe this is simple but effective wisdom to start off with. But it leaves much room for debate when we see those that are in bad movies playing a bad role and calling themselves Christians. Let's take Training Day for example - how is Denzel Washington, a bible quoting, filled with the Holy Spirit Christian, playing a role like that? You may argue with me, but I believe the redemptive thread in the movie was that the good cop won. See how complicated this can be - which is why ultimately I believe wisdom is justified by her children. Let's dig a bit deeper.

God Sends his People into Darkness

The Bible gives us a good point of reference for our involvement and interactions with the world through the lives of Daniel, Joseph and Jesus. They were hidden by God in dark governments to strategically come forth at the time needed. Jesus gives us a good look at this in Matthew.

> **Matthew 13:33** *Another parable He spoke to them: "The kingdom of heaven is like leaven, which a woman took and hid in three measures of meal till it was all leavened."*

Scholars have debated the meaning of this scripture because all other references to leaven have to do with being aware of the wicked doctrine of the Pharisees and Herod, which Jesus called hypocrisy. I will lean towards the side that agrees that in this passage, He clearly refers leaven to the Kingdom of Heaven. I believe the woman is a representation of the church that takes the Kingdom and hides it in the meal; eventually the whole meal is leavened. Let's say it this way: the Kingdom is hidden by us in the church in the world systems of today and will affect the world until all is leavened.

To me, this revelation of Matthew 13:33 explains why Daniel served Nebuchadnezzar, helped interpret his dreams and gave insight for his wicked Kingdom. This truth plays out with Joseph who gave Potiphar the interpretation of a dream to save Egypt (which later would enslave Israel.) Joseph was hidden so much in the culture of Egypt that his own brothers did not recognize him. As we can see, this fit into the plan that God knew would unfold throughout history. How many actors like Denzel Washington, Tyler Perry or Dyan Cannon (who holds Christian meetings on a CBS backlot blasting people with the Holy Spirit) has the body written off? But God hasn't.

Joseph and Paul, who were both used by God, were kept hidden until their own will and agenda was submitted to God. Joseph had a dream of greatness, was thrown into a pit by his brothers, went from the pit to the palace and then to jail. By the time he came on the scene to lead Egypt and his people he was dead to himself. God had worked out the issues in his life so that he could be used in the exact dream he had of greatness. Catch this, until the time that Joseph led his people he made some major mistakes. However, during the times of his mistakes, the Bible continues to say God was with him. There are people in Hollywood who love the Lord and are making some big mistakes, but this does not mean that the Lord is not with them. Paul, who preached in the marketplace and reasoned daily with people to get them saved, didn't start that way. Paul persecuted the very Christians and faith that he would later defend until his death. What a turnaround! God can use anyone! That's exciting, but what I want to show you here is that God sent Joseph into Egypt (like Hollywood) and Paul into the marketplace (like Wall Street) to lead his people out of darkness into the light. Could it be that as Hurricane Entertainment is fiercely blowing across our nation, God has planted people (maybe even you) to move into the storm and then into the eye of the storm - to see how to bring many to him out of darkness and into the light?

If we look through history at how much entertainment has played a major role in the rise and fall and shaping of culture around the world, we have to take notice of the time called the "Renaissance." Renaissance is a French word that means rebirth. It's the time period from the 14th through 17th centuries, right after the Dark Ages. Europe was recovering from the Bubonic Plague that wiped out about 1.2 million people (which was almost half of the 4.2 million population.) During the Renaissance, Humanism became popular - but so did Entertainment.

It's amazing to me that the time known as the rebirth is the time known for an explosion of the Arts, Poetry and Music. Artists like Leonardo da Vinci and Michelangelo rose to fame during the Renaissance. Writers like Sir Phillip Sidney and William Shakespeare also hit the scene during this time. The earth was earnestly waiting for the Sons of God to manifest, the early reformers did arise.

To me, it's no coincidence that the greatest time of enlightenment for Arts and Music is coupled with the greatest time of reformation to the church! People like John Hus and Martin Luther led the charge. Martin Luther was even pushing the reformation of music because he was an artist that understood the power of music. The time of the Renaissance was so influential to Arts and Entertainment that Tupac Shakur, one of Hip Hop's greatest Rappers, changed his name to Machiavelli. Machiavelli was a historian, politician, diplomat, philosopher, humanist and writer, born in Florence, Italy. What is remarkable to me is if you really listen to Tupac, you will hear the spirit of reformation in his lyrics. How many of our athletes, painters, singers, actors, cameramen, writers, etc., are carrying the next Move of God, hidden by the veil of deception, pain, hurt or misunderstanding? I believe that just like the Renaissance (which rebirthed the church by the reformers of that day) the next Move of God will come through the influence of the Arts and Entertainers of our time.

My friends, for those of us called to Entertainment that are not deceived, misunderstood or carrying hurt and pain, God is calling us to go into the world of Entertainment. While others are running around in panic that Hurricane Entertainment is going to sink the boat of our nation, we are resting because we have put our head (our thoughts) to meditating on Christ. We aren't looking at how bad Entertainment is - we see how wonderful it is! We aren't having fits of envy and rage - we are having Joel dreams of Heaven Invading Hollywood! We don't see all the wicked people in Entertainment - we see from God's eye - full of love - all the harvest we are about to bring in! We are getting our hearts so full that whatever set it is, whatever studio, museum, football, soccer or baseball field, basketball or tennis court, fishing stream, art show, stage or arena - we are ready! It doesn't matter what form of Entertainment it is – we are ready! Whenever God yells "Action," we will be ready to stand up and say "Peace be Still!" The Sons of God will cause the winds of Hurricane Entertainment to cease because… **Entertainment is a God Eyedea!**

Notes

About jo'EL

jo'EL is the Apostle of His House International Covenant Church in Oceanside, Ca. He comes from a family with a history of Pastors and Ministers of the Gospel. Together, jo'EL and his wife Lupita lead an amazing group of radical believers on fire to transform Oceanside and change the world. His House is a nondenominational church with a diverse community.

jo'EL is also an Actor, Rapper, Writer and Businessman currently coaching and consulting with Experts 29. Experts 29 is an internet based company showing Christians all around the world how to walk in Outrageous Influence in the 7 Mountains. jo'EL and Lupita have 6 children and 6 grandchildren.

That's a wrap!

34078494R00075

Made in the USA
San Bernardino, CA
18 May 2016